Introducing Blockchain with Lisp

Implement and Extend Blockchains with the Racket Language

Boro Sitnikovski

Apress®

Introducing Blockchain with Lisp: Implement and Extend Blockchains with the Racket Language

Boro Sitnikovski
Skopje, North Macedonia

ISBN-13 (pbk): 978-1-4842-6968-8 ISBN-13 (electronic): 978-1-4842-6969-5
https://doi.org/10.1007/978-1-4842-6969-5

Managing Director, Apress Media LLC: Welmoed Spahr
Acquisitions Editor: Steve Anglin
Development Editor: Matthew Moodie
Coordinating Editor: Mark Powers

Cover designed by eStudioCalamar

Cover image by Michael Dziedzic on Unsplash (www.unsplash.com)

Distributed to the book trade worldwide by Apress Media, LLC, 1 New York Plaza, New York, NY 10004, U.S.A. Phone 1-800-SPRINGER, fax (201) 348-4505, e-mail orders-ny@springer-sbm.com, or visit www.springeronline.com. Apress Media, LLC is a California LLC and the sole member (owner) is Springer Science + Business Media Finance Inc (SSBM Finance Inc). SSBM Finance Inc is a **Delaware** corporation.

For information on translations, please e-mail booktranslations@springernature.com; for reprint, paperback, or audio rights, please e-mail bookpermissions@springernature.com.

Apress titles may be purchased in bulk for academic, corporate, or promotional use. eBook versions and licenses are also available for most titles. For more information, reference our Print and eBook Bulk Sales web page at http://www.apress.com/bulk-sales.

Any source code or other supplementary material referenced by the author in this book is available to readers on GitHub via the book's product page, located at www.apress.com/9781484269688. For more detailed information, please visit http://www.apress.com/source-code.

Printed on acid-free paper

Table of Contents

About the Author

Boro Sitnikovski has over 10 years of experience working professionally as a software engineer. He started programming using the Assembly programming language on an Intel x86 at the age of 10. While in high school, he won several prizes for competitive programming, varying from fourth, third, and first place.

He is an informatics graduate; his Bachelor's thesis was titled "Programming in Haskell Using Algebraic Data Structures," and his Master's thesis was titled "Formal Verification of Instruction Sets in Virtual Machines." He has also published papers on software verification. Other research interests include programming languages, mathematics, logic, algorithms, and writing correct software.

He is a strong believer in the open-source philosophy and contributes to various open-source projects.

In his spare time, he enjoys time with his family.

About the Technical Reviewer

Spiro Buzharovski is a mechanical engineer. For the last several years, he has worked as a full-stack software developer in the IT sector. Prior experience includes more than six years of mechanical engineering work in the oil and gas sector. His interests include Java frameworks, blockchains, and the latest high-tech trends.

Preface

This book aims to be accessible to novices who have some basic working experience with computers, and at least *some* experience with programming. Knowing how to program is not a strict necessity, although it may help in grasping some concepts. The book also assumes some experience with high school mathematics, such as functions.

One of the reasons for writing this book is that I could not find a single book that explained how to implement blockchain from scratch, covering all the details. I had to do a lot of research on the Internet to come up with a complete picture of what blockchain is, how one can implement it, and what it is good for.

Since it's easy to get sidetracked by the amount of information, every chapter contains a summary to serve as recall. Moving back and forth between chapters until information sticks can be useful in aiding understanding.

The recommended approach to the book is to follow along and write the code as it's being explained instead of reading passively. This way you will get the most of it. All of the source code is available for download from `https://github.com/bor0/racket-coin`.

You can access my blog at `https://bor0.wordpress.com` and check out some of my latest work. Feel free to contact me at `buritomath@gmail.com` for any questions you might have, and I will do my best to answer.

Thanks to my family, coworkers, and friends for all the support they give to me.

Finally, thank you for purchasing this book! I hope that you will learn new techniques in reading this book and that it will spark more interest in Lisp and blockchain.

CHAPTER 1

Introduction to Blockchain

The blockchain bazaar, by D. Bozhinovski

© Boro Sitnikovski 2021
B. Sitnikovski, *Introducing Blockchain with Lisp*, https://doi.org/10.1007/978-1-4842-6969-5_1

This chapter introduces some important blockchain definitions and examples. We will see what properties a blockchain has, what it allows us to do, and what it is good for.

---

❶ Definition 1-1

Blockchain is a system in which a record of transactions is maintained across several computers that are linked in a peer-to-peer network.[1]

We will give an example that will serve as a motivation, as well as define what encryption and hashing techniques are and how can they help us with our system.

Note that we will hand-wave some of the technical bits in this chapter, as it serves as introductory material. The technical bits will be uncovered later when we start building the blockchain.

1.1 Motivation and Basic Definitions

Let's assume that you and your friends exchange money often, for example, when paying for dinner or drinks. It can be inconvenient to exchange cash all the time.

One possible solution is to keep records of all the bills that you and your friends have. This is called a *ledger* and is depicted in Figure 1-1.

---

[1]We will use this definition of blockchain throughout the book, but note that there are many different definitions on the Internet. By the end of this book, you should be able to distinguish the slight nuances and similarities in each definition of blockchain.

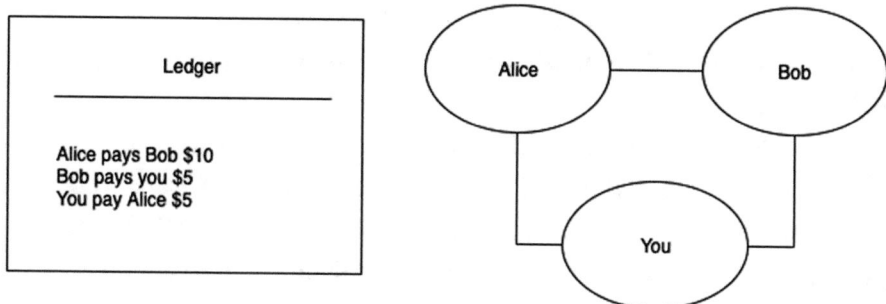

Figure 1-1. *A ledger and a set of connected friends (peers)*

---

❶ Definition 1-2

A **ledger** is a book that contains a record of transactions.

Further, at the end of every day, you all sit together and refer to the ledger to do the calculations to settle up. Let's imagine that there is a pot, which is the place where all of the money is kept. If you spent more than you received, you put money into the pot; otherwise, you take money out.

We want to design a system that functions similarly to a regular bank account. A holder of a wallet (the bank account) should only be able to send money from their wallet to other wallets. Thus, every person in the system will have a *wallet* of a kind, which can also be used to determine their balance. Note that with the current setup using a ledger, we have to go through all existing records to determine the balance of a specific wallet.

If we want to avoid going through all existing records, there is a way we can optimize this, using *unspent transaction outputs* (UTXOs), as we will see in Section 3.5.

A problem that may arise is the so-called *double-spending* problem, where Bob can try to send all of his money to Alice and you at the same time. This would effectively double the money he sends in relation to what he has. There are several ways this can be resolved, and the solution that we will provide will be a simple check of the sum of the inputs and the sum of the outputs (UTXO).

Another problem that might appear with this kind of system is that anyone can add a transaction. For example, Bob can add a transaction in which Alice pays him a few dollars without Alice's approval. We need to rethink our system so that each transaction will be verified/signed.

---

❶ Definition 1-3

A **digital signature** is a way to verify the authenticity of digital messages and documents.

To sign and verify transactions, we will rely on digital signatures (Figure 1-2). For now, let's assume that anyone who adds information to the ledger also adds a signature with each record, and others have no way to modify the signature, but can only verify it. We will cover the technical details in Section 1.2.

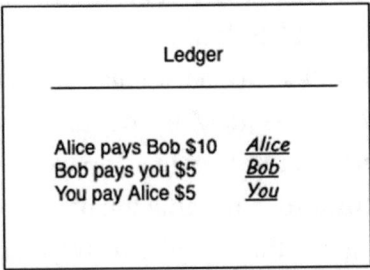

Figure 1-2. *Our ledger now contains signatures*

Now let's assume that Bob is keeping the ledger to himself, and everybody agrees to this. The ledger is now stored in what is called a *centralized place.* If Bob is unavailable at the end of the day when everybody gathers to settle up, nobody will be able to refer to the ledger.

We need to find a way to decentralize the ledger, so that at any given time, anyone can make a transaction. For this, every person involved will keep a copy of the ledger to themselves, and when they meet at the end of the day, they will sync their ledgers.

You are connected to your friends, and so are they to you. Informally, this makes it a peer-to-peer network.

---

❶ Definition 1-4

A **peer-to-peer network** is formed when two or more computers are connected to each other.

For example, when you are accessing a web page on the Internet using a browser, your browser is the "client" and the web page you're accessing is hosted by a "server." This represents a centralized system since every user is getting the information from a single place—the "server."

In contrast, in a peer-to-peer network—which represents a decentralized system—the distinction between a "client" and a "server" is blurred. Every peer is both a "client" and a "server" at the same time.

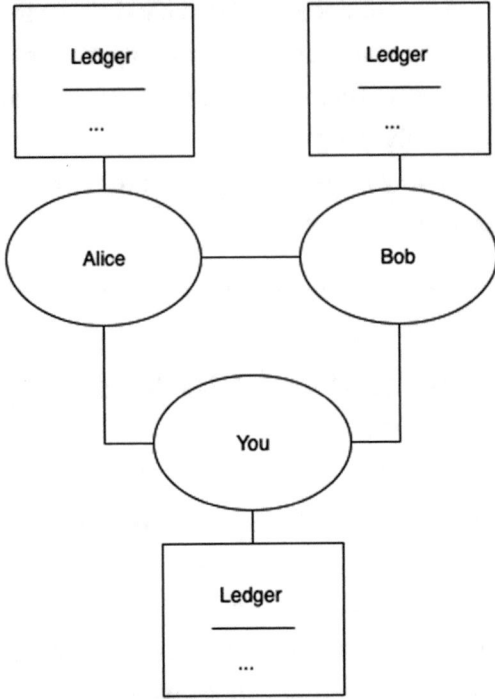

Figure 1-3. *A decentralized ledger*

With a decentralized system (see Figure 1-3), as the list of peers (persons) grows, we might run into a problem of *trust*. When everybody meets at the end of the day to sync their ledgers, how can they believe that the transactions listed in other people's ledgers are true? Even if everybody trusts everybody else's ledger, what if a new person wants to join this network? It's natural for existing users to ask this newcomer to prove that they can be trusted. We need to modify our system to support this kind of trust. One way to achieve that is through a *proof of work*, which we introduce next.

---

❶ Definition 1-5

A **proof of work** is data that is time-consuming to calculate, and easy for others to verify.

For each record we will also include a special number (or a hash) that will represent *proof of work,* in that it will provide proof that the transaction is valid. We will cover the technical details in Section 1.3.

At the end of the day, we agree that we will trust the ledger of the person who has put most of the work in it. If Bob has some errands to run, he can catch up the next day by trusting the rest of the peers in the network.

In addition to all this, we want the transactions to have an order, so every record will also contain a link to the previous record. This represents the actual blockchain, as depicted in Figure 1-4.

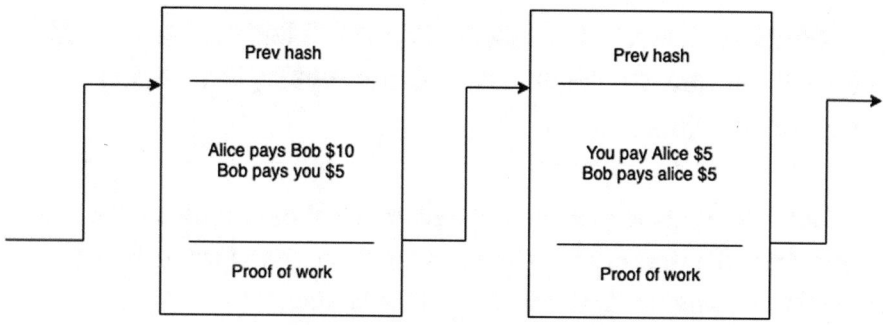

Figure 1-4. A chain of blocks, aptly called a blockchain

If everybody agreed to use this ledger as a source of truth, there would be no need to exchange physical money at all. Everybody can just use the ledger to put money in or retrieve it.

To understand the technical bits of digital signatures and proof of work, we will be looking at encryption and hashing, respectively. Fortunately for us, the programming language that we will be using has built-in functionalities for encryption and hashing. We don't have to dig too deep into how hashing and encryption and decryption work, because a basic understanding will be sufficient.

Observe how we started with a simple definition of a ledger and gradually built up to a complex system. We will use the same approach in programming.

1.2 Encryption

We will start by defining encryption and decryption.

---

❶ Definition 1-6

Encryption is a method of encoding values so that only authorized persons can view the original content. **Decryption** is a method of decoding encrypted values.

Note that in this section we will mostly talk about numbers, but characters and letters can also be encrypted/decrypted using the same methods, by using the ASCII[2] values for the characters.

Before we talk about encryption, we first have to recall what *functions* are, since encoding/decoding values is achieved by using functions.

---

[2]The ASCII table is a table that assigns a unique number to each character (such as !, @, a, Z, etc.).

1.2.1 Functions

Figure 1-5 shows a visual representation of a function. An input goes in the function and an output is produced.

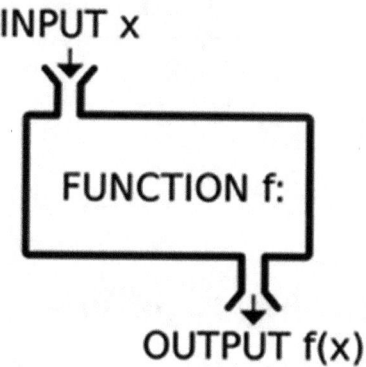

Figure 1-5. *A function*

ⓘ Definition 1-7

Functions are mathematical entities that assign unique outputs to given inputs.

For example, you might have a function that accepts as input a person and then returns the person's age or name as the output. Another example is the function $f(x) = x + 1$. There are many inputs this function can accept: 1, 2, and 3.14. For example, when we input 2 it gives us an output of 3, since $f(2) = 2 + 1 = 3$.

One simple way to think of functions is in the form of tables. For a function $f(x)$ accepting a single argument x, we have a two-column table where the first column is the input and the second column is the output. For a function $f(x, y)$ that's accepting two arguments x and y, we have a three-column table where the first and second columns represent the input, and the third column is the output. Thus, to display the function discussed above in the form of a table, it would look like this:

x	f(x)
1	2
2	3
...	...

1.2.2 Symmetric-Key Algorithm

We can assume that there exist functions $E(x)$ and $D(x)$ for encryption and decryption, respectively. We want these functions to have the following properties:

- $E(x) \neq x$, meaning that the encrypted value should not be the same as the original value.

- $E(x) \neq D(x)$, meaning that the encryption and decryption functions produce different values.

- $D(E(x)) = x$, meaning that the decryption of an encrypted value should return the original value.

For example, let's assume there's some kind of an encryption scheme, say E("Boro") = 426f726f. We can "safely" communicate the value 426f726f without actually exposing our original value, and only those who know the decryption scheme D(x) will be able to see that D(426f726f) = "Boro".

Another example of an encryption scheme is for $E(x)$ to shift every character in x forward, and for $D(x)$ to shift every character in x backward. This scheme is known as the *Caesar cipher*. To encrypt the text "abc" we have E("abc") = "bcd", and to decrypt it, we have D("bcd") = "abc".

However, this scheme makes a *symmetric algorithm*, as shown in Figure 1-6, meaning that we have to share the functions E and D with the parties involved. That makes it open to attacks.

Figure 1-6. *Symmetric-key algorithm*

1.2.3 Asymmetric-Key Algorithm

To solve the problems that arise with symmetric-key algorithms, we will use what is called an *asymmetric algorithm* or *public-key cryptography* (Figure 1-7). In this scheme, we have two kinds of keys: public and private. We share the public key with the world and keep the private one to ourselves.

This algorithm scheme has a neat property in which only the private key can decode a message, and only the public key can encode a message.

We have two functions that should have the same properties as those for the symmetric-key algorithm:

- $E(x, p)$ encrypts a message x given a public key p

- $D(x', s)$ decrypts an encrypted message x' given a private (secret) key s

11

Figure 1-7. *Asymmetric-key algorithm*

In our example, we will rely on the modulo operation. Recall, from high school, that *a* mod *b* represents the remainder when *a* is divided by *b*. For example, 4 mod 2 = 0 because there is no remainder when dividing 4 by 2, however, 5 mod 2 = 1.

Here's one example of a basic encryption algorithm based on addition and modulo operations:

1. Pick one random number, for example 100. This will represent a common, publicly available key.

2. Pick another random number in the range (1, 100), for example, 97. This will represent the private key *s*.

3. The public key *p* is obtained by subtracting the common key from the private one: 100 − 97 = 3.

4. To encrypt data, add it to the public key and the take modulo 100. $E(x, p) = (x + p)$ mod 100.

5. To decrypt data, we use the same logic but with our private key, so $D(x', s) = (x' + s)$ mod 100.

For example, suppose we want to encrypt 5. Then $E(5, 3) = (5 + 3)$ mod 100 = 8. To decrypt 8, we have $D(8, 97) = (8 + 97)$ mod 100 = 105 mod 100 = 5.

This example uses a very simple generation pair: $(x + y)$ mod *c*. But, in practice, the pair-generation algorithm is much more complex and harder for attackers to break. After all, the complexity of the algorithm's computation is what makes it hard to break.

We can use a similar algorithm for digital signatures:

- $S(x, s)$ signs a message x given a private key s (encryption).

- $V(x', sig, p)$ verifies a signed message x', given signature sig and public key p (decryption).

As we said earlier, each record will also include a special number (or a hash). This hash will be what is produced by $S(x, s)$ (encryption), and it can be verified by using the verify function to confirm a record's ownership (decryption).

The wallet will contain a pair of public and private keys. These keys will be used to receive or send money. With the private key, it is possible to write new blocks (or transactions) to the blockchain, effectively spending money. With the public key, others can use it to send money to the wallet and verify signatures.

🖉 Exercise 1-1

Come up with a table of functions such that:

1. The input is a number and the output is a number.

2. The input is a number and the output is the name of an employee in a company given that number.

🖉 Exercise 1-2

Check the three properties for a symmetric-key algorithm to ensure that the Caesar cipher is compatible with them.

🖉 Exercise 1-3

Come up with an encryption scheme, based on mathematical substitution.

✏️ Exercise 1-4

Use the asymmetric-key algorithm we defined to sign a message and verify it.

Hint: This is similar to the encryption/decryption example that we showed.

1.3 Hashing

❶ Definition 1-8

Hashing is a one-way function in that it encodes text without a way to retrieve the original value.

Hashing is simpler than the previously described encryption schemes. One example of a hashing function is to return the length of characters - $H(\text{``abc''}) = 3$, but also $H(\text{``bcd''}) = 3$. This means that we don't have a way to retrieve the original value other than by using the return value 3.

As we mentioned earlier, the reason to use such a technique is that it has some interesting properties, such as providing us with proof of work.

❶ Definition 1-9

Mining is the process of validating transactions. For this effort, successful miners obtain money as a reward.

Hashcash is one kind of a proof of work system.[3] We will use it to implement mining. We will see how this algorithm works in detail in the later chapters, when we implement it.

Hashing functions have another useful property that allows us to connect two or more distinct blocks by having the information about the current block's hash (`current-hash`) and the previous block's hash (`previous-hash`) in each block. For example, `block-1` may have a hash such as 123456 and `block-2` may have a hash such as 345678. Now, `block-2`'s `previous-hash` will be `block-1`'s `current-hash`, that is, 123456. Here, we linked these two blocks, effectively creating a linked list of blocks containing ledgers with transactions. This linking is depicted in Figure 1-4.

The hash of the block is based on the block's data itself, so to verify a hash, we can just hash the block's data and compare it to `current-hash`.

Two or more blocks (or transactions) that are connected form a blockchain. The validity of the blockchain will depend on the validity of each transaction.

✎ Exercise 1-5

Come up with your own hashing function.

✎ Exercise 1-6

How can the linked list depicted in Figure 1-4 be traversed? What are the implications of this property?

---

[3]Hashcash was initially targeted for limiting email spam and other attacks. However, recently it's also become known for its use in blockchains as part of the mining process. Hashcash was proposed in 1997 by Adam Backa.

1.4 Smart Contracts

---

❶ Definition 1-10

A **smart contract** is a self-executing contract in which the conditions of an agreement between a buyer and a seller are directly expressed by lines of code.

A blockchain is programmable if the transaction conditions themselves can be programmed by users. For example, users (not necessarily programmers) can write a script to add requirements that must be satisfied before sending money. It could look something like this:

```
1    if (user has more than 10 money)
2        then approve transaction
3        else reject transaction
```

Smart contracts are implemented as a computation that takes place on the blockchain. We will implement a very basic functionality of smart contracts in the later chapters.

1.5 Bitcoin

Bitcoin was the world's first implementation of a blockchain. In November 2008, a paper authored by Satoshi Nakamoto, entitled "Bitcoin: A Peer-to-Peer Electronic Cash System," was published on a cryptography mailing list. Bitcoin's whitepaper is nine pages, however, it is a mostly theoretical explanation of the design, and as such may be a bit overwhelming to newcomers.

The Bitcoin software is open-source code and was released in January 2009 on SourceForge. The design of a Bitcoin includes a decentralized network (peer-to-peer network), block (mining), blockchain, transactions, and wallets, each of which we will look at in detail in this book.

Although there are many blockchain models and each differs in implementation details, the blockchain we will be building upon in this book will look pretty similar to Bitcoin, with some parts simplified.

1.6 Example Workflows

We will list a few important workflows that our system will use, among others.

Mining a block creates a new block, using Hashcash to calculate the `current-hash` of the block. It also contains `previous-hash`, which is a link to the previous block in the blockchain.

Checking a wallet balance for person A will first filter all blocks in the blockchain (sender = A or receiver = A) and then sum them to calculate the balance. The more our blockchain grows, the longer this operation will take. For that purpose, we will use the unspent transaction outputs (UTXO) model. This model is a list of transactions containing information about the owner and the amount of money. Thus, every transaction will consume elements from this list.

Adding a block to a blockchain consists of sending money from A to B. One prerequisite is that A has enough money. We check this using the wallet balance workflow. We proceed by creating a transaction (sender = A, receiver = B) and signing it. Then we mine a block using this transaction and update the UTXO with the rewards.

1.7 Summary

The point of this chapter is to provide a vague idea of how the system that we will implement looks. Things will become much clearer in the implementation chapter (Chapter 3), where we have to be explicit about the definitions of every component.

Here's briefly what we learned in this chapter:

- The core component of the system is a block.

- A block contains (among other data) transactions.

- We have a ledger that is an ordered list of all valid blocks (a blockchain).

- Every peer involved with the ledger has a wallet.

- Every record in the ledger is signed by the owner and can be verified by the public (digital signatures).

- The ledger is in a decentralized location, that is, everybody has a copy of it.

- Trust is based on proof of work (mining).

CHAPTER 2

Racket Programming Language

Structure, by D. Bozhinovski

© Boro Sitnikovski 2021

B. Sitnikovski, *Introducing Blockchain with Lisp*, https://doi.org/10.1007/978-1-4842-6969-5_2

Now that we have vaguely explained what a blockchain is and how it is useful, the next obvious step is to implement these calculations in a computer, so that they are automatically performed. In this chapter, we introduce a tool that will allow us to implement these calculations exactly.

2.1 Introduction to Lisp

Lisp, originating from 1958, stands for *LIST Processing* and is a family of programming languages. Unlike standard programming languages, it has a fully parenthesized prefix notation. For example, instead of writing 1 + 2, one would write (+ 1 2).

There are many Lisp implementations in the Lisp family. One such implementation is Racket, and we will use it in this book since this implementation is particularly easy for entry-level programmers. The language is used in a variety of contexts such as research, computer science education, and general-purpose programming. It has also been used for commercial projects. One notable example is the Hacker News[1] website, which runs on Arc, a programming language developed in Racket.

Lisp implementations are quite known for their minimalism. Due to this minimalism, building a blockchain (or anything, for that matter) in Lisp will imply that you can do the same in most other programming languages with ease. Lisps favor function composition—chaining two functions together—for example, given $f(x)$ and $g(x)$, one composition is $f(g(x))$. Further in the book, we will see the interesting properties that composition offers and how easily we can maintain and extend our code.

---

[1]https://news.ycombinator.com/

2.1.1 Data Structures and Recursion

There are three important notions in a Lisp:

- *Primitives* or axioms (starting points or building blocks). As an example, the numbers 1, 2, and so on, are something we do not have to implement ourselves since they are already included in the programming language. Another example is operations on numbers, such as + and *.

- *Composition* or a way to compose primitives to do complex calculations. For example, we can combine + and * as follows: 1 + (2 * 3) or in prefix (Lisp) notation: (+ 1 (* 2 3)).

- *Abstraction* or capturing the composition of primitives. For example, if we find ourselves doing a calculation over and over again, it would be good to capture (abstract, or wrap) it in a function that can be easily reused.

We will rely on these concepts repeatedly throughout the book, as they allow us to build complex structures.

---

❶ Definition 2-1

A **data structure** is a collection of values, the relationships among them, and the functions or operations that can be applied to these values.

An example of a data structure is numbers together with the plus and multiplication functions.

From the motivation in the previous chapter we can see the need of forming such a data structure, where, for example, a block is a structure that contains a hash, an owner, and transaction amount.

There are many data structures. An ordered list is one example, representing the numbers (1, 2, 3) in that order. Further, there are operations on lists, such as counting the number of elements, merging two lists, and so on.

We used the numbers 1, 2, and 3 in the previous example of a list—these elements are *primitives*. A list, together with its operations, represents an *abstraction*. Chaining several list operations together represents a *composition*.

Now that we can transform some data structure (by applying operations on it), it would be good to be able to repeatedly transform a data structure according to some specific rules. For example, if we have a blockchain data structure we may want to come up with a way to transform it such that, for example, a new block is inserted in it. This might require applying the same operation several times.

ℹ Definition 2-2

In mathematics and computer science, functions exhibit **recursive** behavior when they can be defined by two properties:

1. A simple base case (or cases)—a terminating case that returns a value without using recursion

2. A rule (or rules) that reduces toward the base case

The most common example of a recursive function is the factorial function, defined as follows:

$$fact(n) = \begin{cases} 1, \text{if } n = 0 \\ n \cdot fact(n-1), \text{otherwise} \end{cases}$$

For example, using substitution we can see that *fact*(3) evaluates to 3 · *fact*(2), which is 3 · 2 · *fact*(1), and finally 3 · 2 · 1 · *fact*(0), which is just 6.

The recursion we just discussed applies the same operation multiple times, and gives the motivation for the next definition.

ℹ Definition 2-3

A **tree** is a hierarchical, recursive data structure that can have two possible values:

1. An empty value

2. A single value, coupled with another two subtrees

A family tree is one example of a tree. Another example of a tree is a binary tree, whereby the left subtree's value is less than the current value and the right subtree's value is greater than the current value:

```
1    2
2   / \
3  1   3
```

Trees are important in Lisps, as they are used to represent a program's structure. We will discuss this more in the next section.

2.1.2 Languages and Syntax

In this section, we take a quick look at the foundations of a Lisp, which will provide a high overview of the ideas behind Lisps.

---

❶ Definition 2-4

A **language** consists of:

1. Symbols, which can be combined into sentences

2. Grammar, which is a set of rules that tells us which sentences are well-formed

---

This definition of a language is also reflected in programming languages, which have a special grammar called the syntax. For example, the C programming language has a special syntax—you have to follow specific rules when writing program statements.

---

❶ Definition 2-5

An **abstract syntax tree** is a tree representation of the abstract syntactic structure of source code written in a programming language.

When you write a program in a programming language, there's an intermediate step that parses the program's source code and derives an abstract syntax tree.

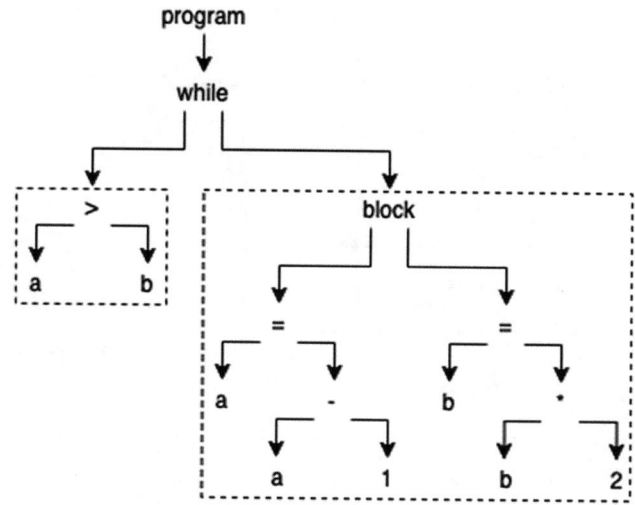

Figure 2-1. *Example 1: Abstract syntax tree*

For example, the image in Figure 2-1 represents an abstract syntax tree for the following pseudocode:

```
1   while (a > b) {
2        a = a - 1;
3        b = b * 2;
4   }
```

As another example, the image in Figure 2-2 represents the following pseudocode:

```
1   if (a == b && b == c) {
2        a = a - 1;
3        b = b * 2;
4   } else a = a * b * 2;
```

It is not important to understand what these codes do, rather understand how such programs are represented internally in programming languages.

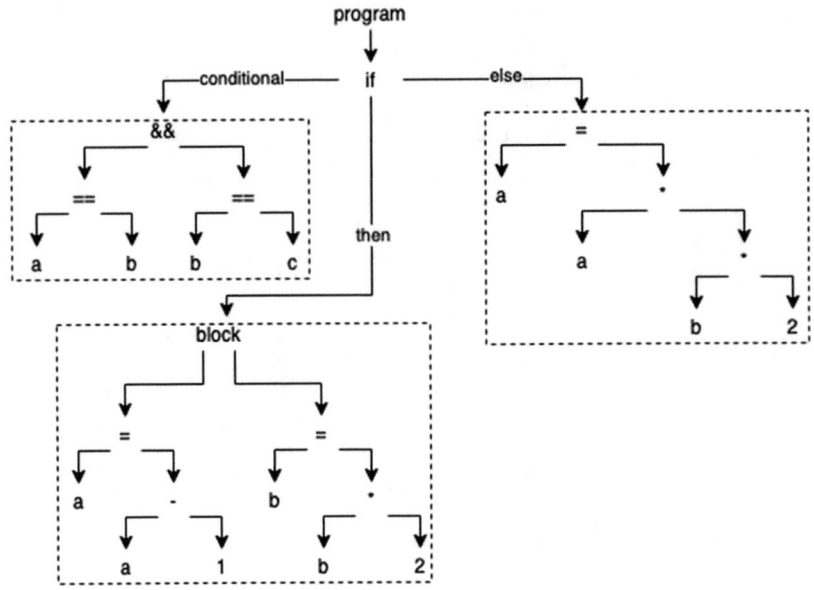

Figure 2-2. *Example 2: Abstract syntax tree*

Lisps do not have the restriction of a special syntax like C has, for example. The code that we will write will be the actual abstract syntax tree. This is why Lisps rely on prefix notation. We see how Lisps are based on a minimalistic design, as we do not get the overhead of many other languages that have special syntax and sometimes functionalities that overlap.

---

❶ Definition 2-6

The syntactic elements in Lisp are symbolic **expressions** or S-expressions. An S-expression can be one of:

1. A symbol (a string of characters)

2. A well-formed list (balanced parentheses) of S-expressions

---

For example, hello is a valid S-expression, and so is (hello there). But (hello(is not a valid S-expression, because the parentheses are not balanced. Whitespace is important in constructing S-expressions. Note that h ello is different from hello.

An S-expression is well-formed if and only if the abstract syntax tree is balanced.

Syntax has a special meaning in Lisps compared to other languages. With macros as part of the core language, it's possible to extend this syntax.[2] S-expressions form the syntax of a Lisp.

✐ Exercise 2-1

We treated numbers with the plus function as a data structure. Think of another data structure.

✐ Exercise 2-2

Evaluate sum(3), sum(5), and sum(1) given the following definition:

$$sum(n) = \begin{cases} 0, \text{if } n = 0 \\ n + sum(n-1), \text{otherwise} \end{cases}$$

What about sum(-1)?

---

[2]We cover more details about macros in Appendix A.

✎ Exercise 2-3

Which of the following S-expressions is valid?

1. `hello`

2. `123`

3. `(hello 123)`

4. `(hello (123)`

5. `(+ 1 (* 2 3))`

6. `(+ (* 3 2) (/ 6 2))`

Hint: Drawing an abstract syntax tree for each of the expressions might make it more obvious why one is or isn't valid.

2.2 Configuration and Installation

Racket can be downloaded and installed via https://download.racket-lang.org. There are binaries available for Windows, Linux, and Mac. This book was written using Racket version 7, but it may work as well with other versions. After downloading and installing the complete package, we can run DrRacket. If you get to the screen shown in Figure 2-3, congratulations! It means that the installation was successful.

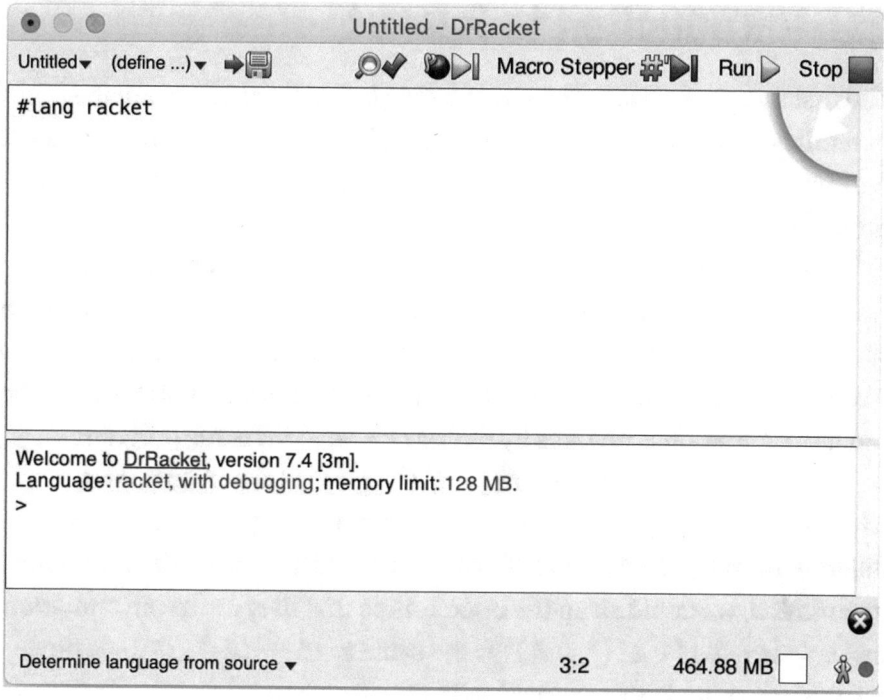

Figure 2-3. *DrRacket*

The upper text area part of the screen is the definitions area, where we usually write the definitions. Alternatively, the lower part is the interactions area, where we interact with the definitions.

The Help Desk, found under Help > Help Desk on the top menu, contains useful information such as a quick introduction, reference manuals, and examples.

There are two main approaches to working with Racket:

- Using the graphical user interface (GUI), which is the recommended way and what we use throughout this book

- Using the command-line utilities (racket is the interpreter/compiler and raco is the package manager), which is for more advanced users

2.3 Introduction to Racket

The first thing that Lisp newcomers notice is that there are too many parentheses in Lisp programs. This is true, but it is a direct consequence of the fact that we are writing our abstract syntax tree in a language that has no special syntax.

As we go through this book, we will see the power of expressiveness we get as a result. For example, one advantage is that there is no need for a special order of operations. In high school, we had to remember that * and / had to be evaluated before + and -. This is not the case with Lisps, as the order of evaluation is obvious by the way we've written our program.

Let's consider the expression (+ 1 (* 2 3)). As we mentioned, whitespace is an important part of S-expressions, so (+1 (* 2 3)) is different from (+ 1 (* 2 3)). To convert this to a more familiar notation in our mind, we could swap the operators so that they are in *infix* notation instead of *prefix*: (+ 1 (* 2 3)) is the same as (1 + (2 * 3)). We now see that the value of this expression is 7.

Next, let's write this expression followed by the return key (Enter) in the interactions area (the bottom text area) of the DrRacket editor:

```
1   > (+ 1 (* 2 3))
2   7
```

The > sign indicates that the command that follows it must be input into the interactions area.

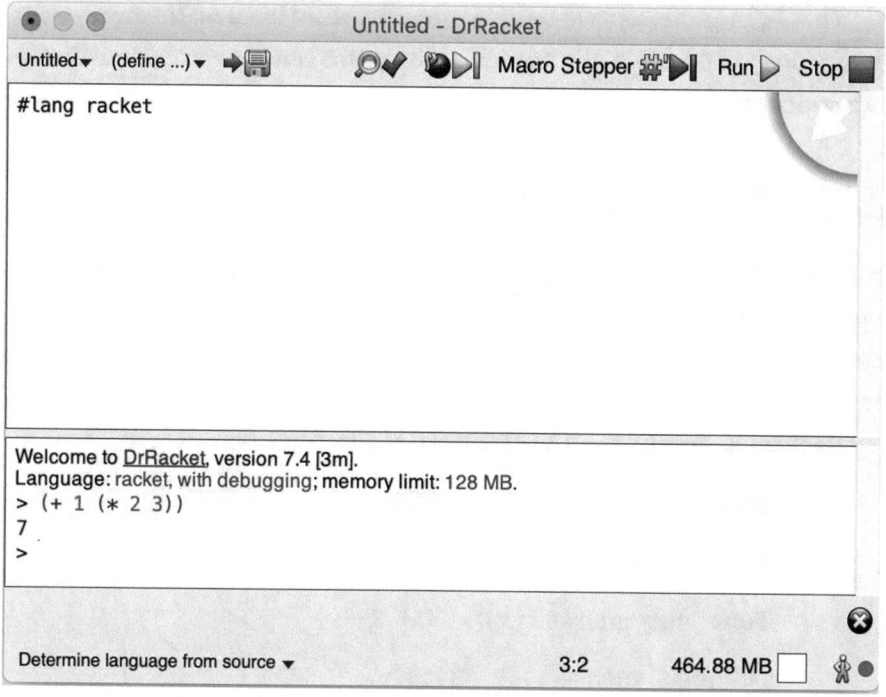

Figure 2-4. *DrRacket first calculation*

We get 7 as a result, as depicted in Figure 2-4. We've done our first calculation in Racket.

After finishing an evaluation, DrRacket again waits for a new command. This is because in the interactions area, we are in REPL mode, which stands for Read-Evaluate-Print-Loop. That is, the interactions area will read what we write, try to evaluate it (come up with a result), print the result, and loop back to reading again.

Lisp evaluation is very similar to substitution in mathematics. For example, one way (+ 1 (* 2 3)) can be evaluated is as follows:

1. (+ 1 (* 2 3))

2. (+ 1 6)

3. 7

That is, in each step, we reduce the expression until no further reductions are possible. We immediately notice how powerful substitution as a concept is.

2.3.1 Primitive Types

In the evaluation above, we got a number as a result—the value 7 has a type of number. While types of values are implicit in Racket, we still have a way to check what the type of a value is, as we will see later with the help of predicates.

Racket has some primitive (built-in) types, such as:

- Symbols, such as hello, world

- Lists, such as (1, 2, 3)

- Functions, such as f(x) = x + 1

- Numbers, such as 1, 2, 3.14

- Booleans, such as #t (for True) and #f (for False)

- Characters or single letters: #\A, #\B, #\C

- Strings or lists of characters: "Hello", "World"

- Bytes: Per ASCII code, we can represent characters in terms of a number (e.g. 72 is H)

- Bytes, as a list of byte: #"Hello", #"World"

```
1   > 123
2   123
3   > #t
4   #t
5   > #f
6   #f
```

```
7    > #\A
8    #\A
9    > "Hello  World"
10   "Hello World"
11   > (bytes 72 101 108 108 111)
12   #"Hello"
```

Each evaluation has a specific type attached to the produced value:

1. The first evaluation (123) has a type of number.

2. The second (#t) and third (#f) evaluations have a type of boolean.

3. The fourth evaluation (#\A) has a type of character.

4. The fifth evaluation ("Hello World") has a type of string.

5. The sixth evaluation ((bytes 72 101 108 108 111)) has a type of bytes and is using the ASCII table for letters.

We cover symbols, lists, and functions in the following sections.

2.3.2 Lists, Evaluation, and Quotes

In order to produce the ordered list (1, 2, 3), we can ask DrRacket to evaluate (list 1 2 3) in the interactions area:

```
1    > (list 1 2 3)
2    '(1 2 3)
```

list is a built-in function, just like +, which we already used. list accepts any number of arguments, and as a result, returns a list generated from them. The returned expression '(1 2 3) is just a fancy notation, which is equivalent to the expression (quote (1 2 3)), where we tell Racket to return the actual list (1 2 3) instead of evaluating it.

We notice how parentheses are used to denote a function call, or evaluation. In general, the code (f a_1 a_2 ... a_n) makes a function call to f, passing n arguments in that order. For example, for the function f(x) = x + 1, one example evaluation is f(1) and we write (f 1), where as a return value we get 2.

Note that (list 1 2 3) returned '(1 2 3) as a result. Let's try to understand what happened here. If (list 1 2 3) had returned (1 2 3), this wouldn't have made much sense since (as we discussed) this notation would try to call the (nonexistent) function 1 with arguments 2 and 3. Instead, it returned a *quoted* list: '(1 2 3).

To understand how this affects evaluation, let's consider an example where you say either of these statements to someone:

- Say your name

- Say "your name"

In the first example, you expect the person to tell you their name. In the second example, you expect them to say the words "your name," rather than their actual name.

Similar to this example, there is a built-in syntax called quote, and we can use it on any set of symbols:

```
1   > (quote hello)
2   'hello
```

This allows for the creation of new symbols and is especially important for the creation of macros. There is a special list, called the *empty list,* and is denoted as (list), or (quote ()), or simply '(). We will later see why this list is special when we start using recursion.

For additional information on list (or any other function), you can click the word using the mouse and press the F1 button. This will open Racket's manuals screen, which will allow you to pick a function that you want information about. Usually, it's the first match on this list. Clicking it should show something similar to Figure 2-5.

```
(list v ...) → list?                                              procedure
  v : any/c
```

Returns a newly allocated list containing the *vs* as its elements.

Examples:

```
> (list 1 2 3 4)
'(1 2 3 4)
> (list (list 1 2) (list 3 4))
'((1 2) (3 4))
```

Figure 2-5. *Racket manual for* list

In Racket, parentheses, brackets, and braces have the same effect. Thus, (list 1 2 3) is the same as [list 1 2 3] and {list 1 2 3}. This visual distinction may be useful to group evaluations when there are a lot of parentheses.

Recall that S-expressions can be either a symbol or a list. Since we discussed evaluation, lists, and symbols in this section, at this point in the book we have covered what makes the core of a Lisp.

✎ Exercise 2-4

Create a list in Racket that contains a mixture of different types (numbers, strings). The list should have at least two elements.

✎ Exercise 2-5

Note that list is a function and quote is a syntax. Read the manual for both using the F1 key.

2.3.3 Dotted Pairs

Another built-in function is cons, which stands for *construct*. This function accepts only two arguments, and as a result, it returns a (quoted) pair:

```
1  > (cons 1 2)
2  '(1 . 2)
```

Think of '(1 . 2) as a sequence of two numbers: 1 and 2.

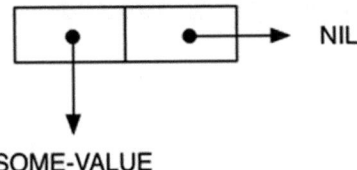

SOME-VALUE

Figure 2-6. *The* (cons 'some-value 'nil) *pair*

There are two other built-in functions, called car and cdr, which are used to retrieve the first and the second element of a pair, respectively:

```
1  > (car (cons 1 2))
2  1
3  > (cdr (cons 1 2))
4  2
5  > (car '(1 . 2))
6  1
7  > (cdr '(1 . 2))
8  2
```

Note how we used function composition here, namely, we "composed" car and cons in the first example, and cdr and cons in the second example.

Pairs are so important that we can encode any data structure with them. In fact, lists are a special kind of pair, where (list 1 2 3) is equal to (cons 1 (cons 2 (cons 3 '()))). See Figure 2-7.

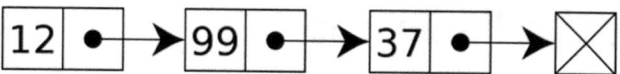

Figure 2-7. *An example of a list*

The motivation for using a list is that it will allow us, for example, to link several blocks together to make a blockchain.

Racket also supports sets. In a list/pair there can be repeated elements, but in a set all elements are unique. Additionally, there are operations that we can use on sets, such as union (merges two sets), subtraction (removes the elements in set 1 that are found in set 2), and so on.

For example, consider the following code where the built-in functions list->set, set-union, and set-subtract are used:

```
1   > (list->set '(1 2 3 4 4))
2   (set 1 3 2 4)
3   > '(1 2 3 4 4)
4   '(1 2 3 4 4)
5   > (set-union (list->set '(1 2 3)) (list->set '(3 4 5)))
6   (set 1 5 3 2 4)
7   > (set-subtract (list->set '(1 2 3)) (list->set '(3 4 5)))
8   (set 1 2)
```

We notice how in Lisp, depending only on a few primitive notions (function calls, pairs, and quote), we can capture abstraction. We will talk more about this in Section 2.3.13.

✎ Exercise 2-6

Represent the same list you created in Exercise 2-4 using cons.

✎ Exercise 2-7

Use a combination of car and cdr for the list in Exercise 2-6 to get the second element in the list.

2.3.4 Adding Definitions

So far we've worked only with the interactions area in DrRacket. Let's try to do something useful with the definitions area.

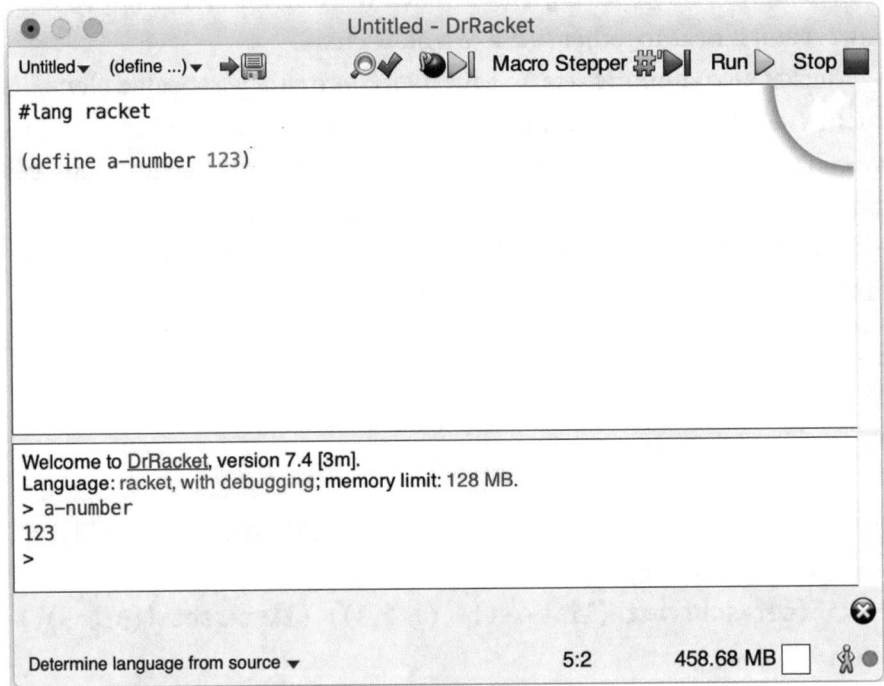

Figure 2-8. *Adding definitions in DrRacket*

We can notice a couple of things in the screenshot in Figure 2-8:

- In the definitions area, we added some code. We notice that we used another built-in syntax named define to attach a value (123) to a symbol/variable (a-number).

- In the interactions area, we interacted with something that was already defined in the definitions area. In this case, the interaction was to just display the definition's value by referring to its symbol.

In this book, every Racket program will start with #lang racket. This means that we will be dealing with Racket's ordinary syntax. There are different values this can accept; for example, we can work with a language specialized in drawing graphics, but that is out of context for this book.

Everything that we write in the definitions area we can also write in the interactions area and vice versa. To have the definitions available in the interactions area, we need to run the program by choosing Racket > Run from the top menu. Note that when we run a program, the interactions area gets cleared.

If our definitions have references to other definitions, we can hover over the symbol's name using the mouse and DrRacket will draw a line pointing to the definition of that reference (Figure 2-9). For big and complex programs, this will be useful for uncovering details of a function.

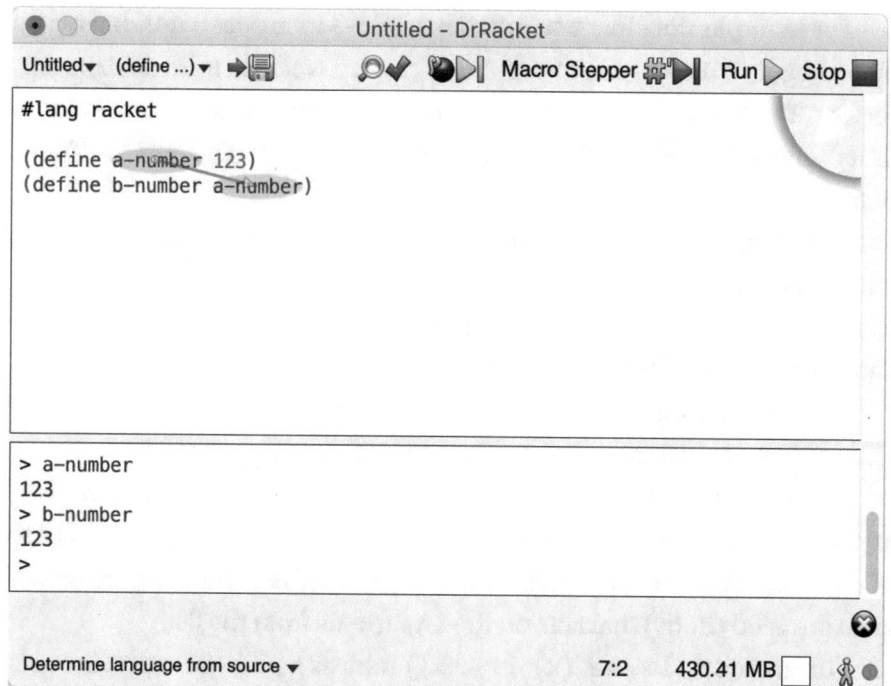

Figure 2-9. *Following references in DrRacket*

Definitions can be saved to a file for later usage by choosing File > Save Definitions from the top menu.

✏ Exercise 2-8

Store the list from Exercise 2-7 in the definitions area and then use car and cdr on that list in the interactions area.

2.3.5 Procedures and Functions

In Lisp, a procedure is essentially a mathematical function. When called, it returns some data. However, unlike mathematical functions, some Lisp expressions and procedures have side effects.

For example, consider two functions: add-1 increases a number by one and get-current-weather gets the current weather from an external service. The first function will always return the same value at any point in time, whereas the second "function" can return different values at different points in time.

Thus Lisp procedures are not always functions in the "pure" sense of mathematics, but in practice, they are frequently referred to as "functions" anyway (even those that may have side effects), to emphasize that a computed result is always returned.

Given the reasoning in the previous paragraph, from this point, we will refrain from using the word "function" and stick with "procedure."

There is special built-in syntax called lambda, which accepts two arguments and produces a procedure as a result. The first argument is a list of arguments that the procedure will accept, and the second argument is an expression (body) that acts on the arguments from the list.

For example, (lambda (x) (+ x 1)) returns a procedure that accepts a single argument x, such that when this procedure is called with an argument, it increases this argument's value by one: (+ x 1).

Evaluating this expression gives us:

```
1   > (lambda (x) (+ x 1))
2   #<procedure>
```

In order to call the procedure, we can try to pass an argument:

```
1   > ((lambda (x) (+ x 1)) 1)
2   2
```

Of course, writing and evaluating procedures this way is hard. Instead, we can define the procedure in the definitions area and then interact with it in the interactions area:

```
1   (define add-one (lambda (x) (+ x 1)))
```

Interaction:

```
1   > (add-one 1)
2   2
3   > (add-one 2)
4   3
5   > (add-one (add-one 1))
6   3
```

To make things a little bit easier, Racket has special syntax for defining procedures, so these two are equivalent:

```
(define add-one (lambda (x) (+ x 1))) <=> (define (add-one x)
(+ x 1))
```

Procedures can also take more than one argument:

```
(define add (lambda (x y) (+ x y))) <=> (define (add x y)
(+ x y))
```

✎ Exercise 2-9

In Exercise 2-7 you retrieved the second element from a list with
(car (cdr l)). Define a procedure that accepts a list and returns
the second element from that list.

2.3.6 Conditional Procedures

There are useful built-in procedures such as checking whether a value is a
number, whether one number is greater than another, and so on.

```
1   > (number? 1)
2   #t
3   > (number? "hello")
4   #f
5   > (character? #\A)
6   #t
7   > (string? "hello")
8   #t
9   > (byte? 72)
10  #t
11  > (bytes? #"Hello")
12  #t
13  > (procedure? add-one)
14  #t
15  > (symbol? (quote hey))
16  #t
17  > (symbol? 1)
18  #f
19  > (> 1 2)
20  #f
```

```
21   > (= 1 2)
22   #f
23   > (= 1 1)
24   #t
```

if is a built-in syntax that allows the evaluation of expressions based on the *truthiness* of some predicate. It accepts three arguments:

- Conditional to check

- Expression to evaluate if the conditional is true

- Expression to evaluate if the conditional is false

Here's example usage:

```
1   > (if (= 1 1) "It is true" "It is not true")
2   "It is true"
3   > (if (= 1 2) "It is true" "It is not true")
4   "It is not true"
```

The more general syntax for if is cond:

```
1   (cond (test-1 action-1)
2          (test-2 action-2)
3          ...
4          (test-n action-n))
```

Optionally, the last test can be an else to use the specific action if none of the conditions match.

As an example, here is one way to use cond in a definition:

```
1   (define (is-large x)
2     (cond ((> x 10) #t)
3            (else #f)))
```

Interacting with it:

```
1   > (is-large 5)
2   #f
3   > (is-large 10)
4   #f
5   > (is-large 11)
6   #t
```

As we've seen, = is an equality predicate that checks whether two numbers are equal. However, it only works on numbers, and it will raise an error if we use it on anything else:

```
1   > (= 1 2)
2   #f
3   > (= 3.14 3.14)
4   #t
5   > (= '() '())
6   =: contract violation
```

There are three other important equality predicates:

- eq? checks whether two arguments refer to the same object in memory.

- eqv? is the same as eq?, except that it can also be used for primitive types (e.g. numbers, strings).

- equal? is the same as eqv?, except that it can also be used to check if the arguments have the same recursive structure (e.g. lists).

Note that there's only one empty list '() in memory,[3] so all three predicates will return the same value when checking against empty lists.

To show where eq? fails, we will use a built-in procedure called integer->char that converts a number to a character, per ASCII.

```
1   > (integer->char 65)
2   #\A
3   > (eq? '() '())
4   #t
5   > (eq? (integer->char 65) (integer->char 65))
6   #f
7   > (eq? '(1) '(1))
8   #f
```

As expected, this will return true for the empty list but cannot compare objects that aren't referring to the same memory location or lists that actually have elements.

Note how eqv? differs in this case:

```
1   > (eqv? '() '())
2   #t
3   > (eqv? (integer->char 65) (integer->char 65))
4   #t
5   > (eqv? '(1) '(1))
6   #f
```

Finally, equal? will compare structures recursively, supporting lists:

```
1   > (equal? '() '())
2   #t
```

---

[3]The empty list doesn't exist in memory, but a pointer to the memory location 0 is considered the empty list.

```
3    > (equal? (integer->char 65) (integer->char 65))
4    #t
5    > (equal? '(1) '(1))
6    #t
```

✏ Exercise 2-10

We already defined is-large using the cond syntax. Represent it using the if syntax.

✏ Exercise 2-11

Represent the following logic using cond: return 'foo if the value is a string or a number, and 'bar otherwise.

2.3.7 Recursive Procedures

Procedures, just like data structures (e.g. trees), can be recursive. We already saw an example with the factorial procedure, in that it called itself to make a computation or a loop.

For example, here's how we could define a factorial in Racket:

```
1    (define (fact n)
2      (if (= n 0)
3          1
4          (* n (fact (- n 1)))))
```

Calling it will produce the following:

```
1    > (fact 3)
2    6
3    > (fact 0)
4    1
```

For a more advanced example, we will define a procedure that calculates the length (number of elements) of a list:

```
1    (define (list-length x)
2      (cond ((eq? x '()) 0)
3            (else (+ 1 (list-length (cdr x))))))
```

We defined a procedure called list-length that accepts a single argument x and the body of the procedure has the condition:

1. For the empty list, just return 0 since the length of an empty list is 0.

2. Otherwise, return the value of one plus (list-length (cdr x)).

Testing it with a few values:

```
1    > (list-length '(1 2 3))
2    3
3    > (list-length '())
4    0
5    > (list-length '(1))
6    1
```

Recall that lists are represented in terms of pairs:

```
1    > (car '(1 2 3))
2    1
3    > (cdr '(1 2 3))
4    '(2 3)
5    > (car (cdr '(1 2 3)))
6    2
7    > (cdr (cdr '(1 2 3)))
8    '(3)
```

In other words, cdr of a list will return that same list without the first element. Here is how Racket evaluates (list-length '(1 2 3)):

```
1   (list-length '(1 2 3))
2   = (+ 1 (list-length '(2 3)))
3   = (+ 1 (+ 1 (list-length '(3))))
4   = (+ 1 (+ 1 (+ 1 (list-length '()))))
5   = (+ 1 (+ 1 (+ 1 0)))
6   = (+ 1 (+ 1 1))
7   = (+ 1 2)
8   = 3
```

We just saw an example of a recursive behavior, since the recursive cases were reduced to the base case to get a result. With this example, we can see the power of recursion and how it allows us to process values in a repeating manner.

There is another way that we can write list-length:

```
1   > (define (list-length-iter x n)
2       (cond ((eq? x '()) n)
3             (else (list-length-iter (cdr x) (+ n 1)))))
4   > (list-length-iter '(1 2  3) 0)
5   3
```

Here's how it evaluates:

```
1   (list-length-iter '(1 2 3) 0)
2   = (list-length-iter '(2 3) 1)
3   = (list-length-iter '(3) 2)
4   = (list-length-iter  '() 3)
5   = 3
```

Both procedures are recursive, in that they generate the same result. However, the nature of the evaluation is very different.

ℹ Definition 2-7

Recursive procedures can generate an **iterative** or a **recursive** process:

1. A recursive process is one where the current state of calculation is not captured by the arguments, and so it relies on "deferred" evaluations

2. An iterative process is where the current state of calculation is captured completely by its arguments

---

In the previous examples, `list-length` generates a recursive process since it needs to go down to the base case and then build its way back up to do the calculations that were "deferred." In contrast, `list-length-iter` generates an iterative process, since the results are captured in the arguments.

This distinction is important because the very different nature of evaluation implies a few things. For example, iterative processes evaluate faster than recursive ones.

In contrast, some algorithms cannot be written using iterative processes, as we will see later with left and right folds.

✎ Exercise 2-12

The way we implemented `fact` represents a recursive procedure that generates a recursive process. Rework it so that it is still a recursive procedure and generates an iterative process.

2.3.8 Procedures That Return Procedures

We can construct procedures that return other procedures as a result. For example:

```
1  > (define (f x) (lambda (y) (+ x y)))
2  > f
3  #<procedure:f>
4  > (f 1)
5  #<procedure>
6  > ((f 1) 2)
7  3
```

Note the new syntax on line 3. It states that the return value of the expression on the previous line is a procedure named f. However, on line 4, when we execute (f 1), we get an unnamed procedure. That is because lambdas are anonymous functions without a name.

This concept is so powerful that we can implement our own cons, car, and cdr:

```
1  (define (my-cons x y) (lambda (z) (if (= z 1) x y)))
2  (define (my-car z) (z 1))
3  (define (my-cdr z) (z 2))
```

Evaluating:

```
1  > (my-cons 1 2)
2  #<procedure>
3  > (my-car (my-cons 1 2))
4  1
5  > (my-cdr (my-cons 1 2))
6  2
```

Note how we define my-cons to return another procedure that accepts an argument z, and then based on that argument's value, we return either the first or the second element.

Using the substitution method, (my-cons 1 2) evaluates to (lambda (z) (if (= z1 2)). So, this lambda (procedure) "captures" data in a sense. Then, when we call my-car or my-cdr on this procedure, we just pass 1 or 2 to get the first or the second value, respectively.

✎ Exercise 2-13

Implement a procedure so that when it's evaluated, it returns a procedure that returns a constant number.

Hint: (lambda () 1) is a procedure that accepts no arguments and returns a constant number.

2.3.9 General Higher-Order Procedures

With the example above, we've seen how Racket can return procedures as return values (output). However, it can also accept procedures as arguments (input).

ℹ Definition 2-8

A **higher-order procedure** takes one or more procedures as arguments or returns a procedure as a result.

There are three common built-in higher-order procedures: map, filter and fold.

For the purpose of this example, we will rely on these definitions:

```
1    (define my-test-list '(1 2 3))
2    (define (add-one x) (+ x 1))
3    (define (gt-1 x) (> x 1))
```

map takes as input a procedure with a single argument and a list, and it returns a list where all members of the list have this procedure applied to them:

```
1    > (map (lambda (x) (+ x 1)) my-test-list)
2    '(2 3 4)
3    > (map  add-one  my-test-list)
4    '(2 3 4)
```

If we use substitution on (map add-one my-test-list), we get (list (add-one 1) (add-one 2) (add-one 3)). However, it is best to implement these procedures ourselves to understand how they work. map takes a transformation procedure f, together with a list l. We have two cases to cover:

- For the empty list, we just return the empty list.

- Otherwise, we extract the first element, apply the transformation procedure, and reconstruct the list by recursively mapping the remainder of the elements.

```
1    (define (my-map f l)
2      (cond ((eq? l '()) '())
3            (else (cons (f (car l)) (my-map f (cdr l))))))
```

Another higher-order procedure, filter, takes as input a predicate with a single argument and a list, and it only returns those members in the list whose predicate evaluates to true:

```
1    > (filter gt-1 my-test-list)
2    '(2 3)
```

To reimplement `filter`, note that it takes a predicate p, together with a list l. There are three cases:

- For the empty list, just as before, we just return the empty list.

- Otherwise, if a predicate matches the current element, we include it in the generation of the new list, recursively filtering the remainder of the elements.

- Otherwise, we recursively filter the remainder of the elements, skipping the addition of the current one to the list.

```
1  (define (my-filter p l)
2    (cond ((eq? l '()) '())
3          ((p (car l)) (cons (car l) (my-filter p (cdr l))))
4          (else (my-filter p (cdr l)))))
```

Finally, `fold` takes as input a combining procedure that accepts two arguments (the current value and accumulator), an initial value, and a list. `fold` then returns a value combined with this procedure. There are two types of folds, a right and a left one, which combine from the right and the left respectively:

```
1  > (foldr cons '() '(1 2 3))
2  '(1 2 3)
3  > (foldl cons '() '(1 2 3))
4  '(3 2 1)
```

foldr takes a combining operator (procedure) op, together with an initial value i and list l. The two cases we need to cover are as follows:

- For the empty list, we return the initial value.

- Otherwise, we use the combining operator to the current element, applied to the folded remainder of the list.

```
1    (define (my-foldr op i l)
2      (cond ((eq? '() l) i)
3            (else (op (car l)
4                      (my-foldr op i (cdr l))))))
```

foldl is a bit different. We start by defining a procedure that has two cases:

- For the empty list, we return the initial value.

- Otherwise, we call the fold again, changing the initial value to be combined with the current element and the remainder of the list.

```
1    (define (my-foldl op i l)
2      (cond ((eq? '() l) i)
3            (else (my-foldl op (op (car l) i) (cdr l)))))
```

This procedure works in a similar way to foldr, except that the result is captured in the procedure's argument. For example, here's how it unfolds for (my-foldl + 0 '(1 2 3)):

```
1    (my-foldl + 0 '(1 2 3))
2    = (my-foldl + 1 '(2 3))
3    = (my-foldl + 3 '(3))
4    = (my-foldl + 6 '())
5    = 6
```

Note that the right fold exhibits a recursive process (think my-length), while the left one exhibits an iterative process (think my-length-iter).

✏ Exercise 2-14

Implement a procedure so that it calls a procedure that's passed in the arguments.

Hint: (... (lambda () 1)) should return 1.

✏ Exercise 2-15

Use DrRacket's feature to follow definitions on my-map, my-filter, my-foldr, and my-foldl to get a better understanding of how they work.

✏ Exercise 2-16

Pick some operators and predicates and use my-map, my-filter, my-foldr, and my-foldl with them on lists to see what they evaluate to.

2.3.10 Packages

---

❶ Definition 2-9

A **package** in Racket resembles a set of definitions someone has written for others to use.

For example, if we want to use hashing procedures, we would pick a package that implements these and use them. This allows us to put our focus on the system design instead of defining everything from scratch.

Packages can be browsed at https://pkgs.racket-lang.org. They can be installed from the DrRacket GUI. When we try to use a package, we will be provided with an option to install it, given it is available in the packages repository. Alternatively, packages can be installed using raco pkg install <package_name> from the command line. We will take advantage of packages later.

To export objects (variables, procedures, etc.) from a package, we use the provide syntax. As an example, let's create a few procedures and then save their definitions in a file called utils.rkt by choosing File > Save Definitions from the top menu.

```
1   (define (sum-list l) (foldl + 0 l))
2   (define (add-one x) (+ x 1))
3
4   (provide sum-list)
```

We will create another file called test.rkt in the same folder as utils.rkt. We will use the require syntax:

```
1   (require "utils.rkt")
2
3   (define (add-two x) (+ x 2))
```

We can now interact with test.rkt:

```
1   > (sum-list '(1 2 3))
2   6
3   > (add-two 1)
4   3
5   > (add-one 1)
6   add-one: undefined;
```

Note that add-one was undefined because only the procedures we provide in the special syntax (provide ...) will be available for use by those that require the package.

2.3.11 Scope

As a start, let's consider the following definitions:

```
1  (define my-number 123)
2  (define (add-to-my-number x) (+ my-number x))
```

We created a variable called my-number and assigned the number 123 to it. We also created a procedure called add-to-my-number, which adds a number (that's passed to it as an argument) to my-number.

---

❶ Definition 2-10

Scope refers to the visibility of some specific definitions, or to which parts of the program can use these definitions.

---

my-number is defined at the same "level" as add-to-my-number, so it is in the scope of add-to-my-number. But the x in add-to-my-number is only accessible in the body of the procedure definition and not accessible to anything outside it.

Using the let syntax, we can introduce variables that are visible only in a certain section:

```
1  (let ([var-1 value-1]
2        [var-2 value-2])
3  ... our code ...)
```

This creates variables var-1 and var-2, which are visible only in the our code part.

```
1    > (let ((x 1) (y 2)) (+ x y))
2    3
3    > x
4    . . x: undefined;
5    > y
6    . . y: undefined;
```

The letrec syntax which is very similar to let, where in addition the variables will be visible in the variable scope:

```
1    > (letrec ((x 1) (y (+ x 1))) y)
2    2
```

Definition 2-11

🛈 **Variable "shadowing"** occurs when a variable defined in scope has the same name as a variable defined in an outer scope.

For example, compare the result of these two evaluations:

```
1    > (let ((x 1)) x)
2    1
3    > (let ((x 1)) (let ((x 2)) x))
4    2
```

In the second example, we have a let within a let. The inner let is defining an x and so is the outer let. However, the x within the inner let will be used in the inner let's body.

Finally, let's consider another example:

```
1   (define a-number 3)
2   (define (test-1 x) (+ a-number x))
3   (define (test-2 a-number) (+ a-number a-number))
```

Interacting:

```
1   > (test-1 4)
2   7
3   > (test-2 4)
4   8
```

test-1 is using a-number from the global scope. test-2 is using variable shadowing for my-number, so it is the same as saying (define (test-2 x) (+ x x)).

✏ Exercise 2-17

Use DrRacket's feature to follow definitions on test-1 and test-2.

2.3.12 Mutation

---

❶ Definition 2-12

Mutation allows a variable to be redefined with a different value.

Mutation can be achieved using the set! syntax. Consider the following definition:

```
1    (define x 123)
2    x
3    (define x 1234)
4    x
```

This definition will produce an error that says module: identifier already defined in: x. However, the next definition:

```
1    (define x 123)
2    x
3    (set! x 1234)
4    x
```

Will happily print 123 followed by 1234.

Even though mutation looks powerful, good Lisp practice says to avoid mutation when possible. The reason for that is that mutation causes side effects, and side effects make reasoning about programs harder. To demonstrate this issue, consider this definition:

```
1    (define some-number 123)
2
3    (define (add-one)
4      (+ 1 some-number))
5
6    (define (add-one-mutation)
7      (begin
8        (set! some-number (+ 1 some-number))
9        some-number))
```

begin allows us to sequence multiple expressions, executing them in order.

Now let's interact with it:

```
1  > (add-one)
2  124
3  > (add-one)
4  124
```

So far, so good. No side effects, since add-one returns the same value every time it's called. However:

```
1  > (add-one-mutation)
2  124
3  > (add-one-mutation)
4  125
5  > (add-one)
6  126
```

This is what makes it hard to reason about programs—when some of the values are modified, some procedures might return different values for the same inputs. Thus, care must be taken when using mutation. However, we will use mutation in the peer- to-peer implementation later, which will make things slightly simpler.

2.3.13 Structures

---

❶ Definition 2-13

A **structure** is a composite data type that defines a grouped list of variables to be placed under one name.

In Racket, the special syntax struct allows us to capture data structures and come up with a new kind of abstraction. In a sense, we already know how we can capture abstractions with car, cons, and cdr. However, struct is much more convenient since it automatically provides procedures to construct a data type and retrieve its values.

Consider the following example code:

```
1   (struct document (author title content))
2   (define a-document
3     (document
4       "Boro Sitnikovski"
5       "Introducing Blockchain with Lisp"
6       "Hello  World"))
```

From the expression on line 1, we automatically get the following procedures:

- document-author, document-title, document-content extracts values from objects.

- document constructs an object of such type.

- document? checks whether a given object is of such type.

Then, using document on line 3, we can construct an object that is using this data structure.

Next, we can use the automatically generated procedures to extract values from objects that are using this data structure:

```
1   > (document-author a-document)
2   "Boro Sitnikovski"
3   > (document-title a-document)
4   "Introducing Blockchain with Lisp"
5   > (document-content a-document)
6   "Hello World"
```

```
7   > (document? a-document)
8   #t
9   > (document? "test")
10  #f
```

There is also a way to declare mutable structures as follows:

```
1   (struct document (author title content) #:mutable)
```

The #:mutable keyword will automatically generate set-<field>! procedures for every property in the structure.

Now we can interact as follows:

```
1   > (document-author a-document)
2   "Boro Sitnikovski"
3   > (set-document-author! a-document "Boro")
4   > (document-author  a-document)
5   "Boro"
```

✎ Exercise 2-18

Create a person structure that contains a first name, last name, and age.

2.3.14 Threads

---

❶ Definition 2-14

A **thread** is a sequence of instructions that can execute in parallel.

Racket has a built-in procedure thread that accepts a procedure that will run in parallel without blocking the next instruction in order.

We will show an example of demonstrating threads. We will implement a procedure called detailed-fact that will be similar to fact, but also print whatever it is currently processing.

```
1   (define (detailed-fact n)
2     (begin
3       (display "Calculating factorial of ")
4       (displayln n)
5       (if (= n 0)
6           1
7           (* n (detailed-fact (- n 1))))))
```

display is a procedure that prints some text, and displayln is the same, but it also prints a newline.

```
1   > (begin (detailed-fact 1) (detailed-fact 2))
2   Calculating factorial of 1
3   Calculating factorial of 0
4   Calculating factorial of 2
5   Calculating factorial of 1
6   Calculating factorial of 0
```

This code represents a sequential execution and the results make sense. However, we now turn to parallel execution to see what will happen:

```
1   > (begin (thread (lambda () (detailed-fact 1))) (thread
    (lambda ()
2     (detailed-fact 2))))
3   Calculating factorial of 2
4   Calculating factorial of 1
5   Calculating factorial of 0
6   Calculating factorial of 1
7   Calculating factorial of 0
```

Note how we used (thread (lambda () ...)) instead of just (thread ...). As we said, thread expects a procedure, but at the end of the evaluation, there would be the output of factorial of some number (for example 3), so (thread 3) does not make sense.

In this parallel execution, the output is not ordered as it was in the previous case. This means that the lambdas within thread are being executed in parallel, so the order of execution cannot be guaranteed.

We will use threads for parallel processing in the peer-to-peer implementation later, where we will have one thread per peer so that when we are serving one peer we don't block the serving of other peers.

2.4 Creating an Executable

The idea behind producing an executable is so that you can run it on other computers without requiring a DrRacket installation, and also without having to share the original code. In the later chapters, we will create an executable so that the blockchain can be used and shared by others.

To create an example executable, we start with the following code:

```
1   #lang racket
2   (print "Hello")
3   (read-bytes-line)
```

This code will just print the text Hello. The print procedure prints some text (similar to display), and read-bytes-line waits for user input. If we did not use read-bytes-line, it would just print and exit right away, before we could read the text.

Next, we choose Racket > Create Executable. Select Distribution and choose Create. After doing that, the executable should be created in the target folder.

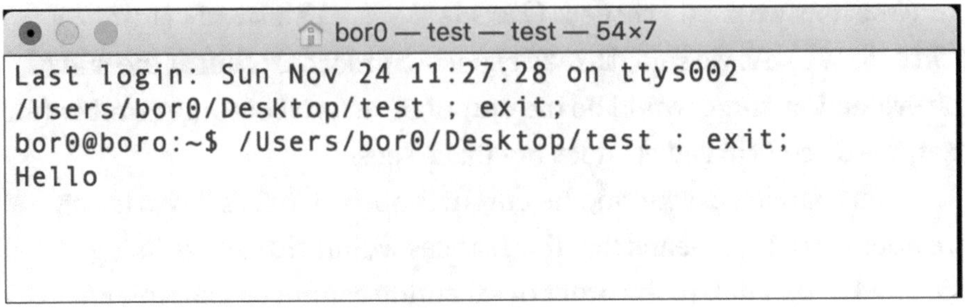

```
● ● ●                🏠 bor0 — test — test — 54×7
Last login: Sun Nov 24 11:27:28 on ttys002
/Users/bor0/Desktop/test ; exit;
bor0@boro:~$ /Users/bor0/Desktop/test ; exit;
Hello
```

Figure 2-10. *Running an executable*

Running the executable should show something similar to Figure 2-10. Pressing the Return key will exit the program.

2.5 Summary

The point of this chapter is to get a basic understanding of the Racket programming language. Here's what we learned in this chapter:

- Lisp is a family of programming languages and Racket belongs to the Lisp family.

- Lisps have no special syntax compared to standard programming languages and syntax is defined differently in Lisp, through S-expressions.

- Lisp evaluation is very similar to substitution in mathematics.

- There are several primitive types: symbols, booleans, characters, strings, and lists.

- Lists are special kinds of pairs.

- Procedures are a way to capture abstraction. They can accept and return any kind of type, including procedures themselves. They can also be recursive.

- Packages allow us to reuse code, written either by ourselves or by someone else.

- Produced executables can be shared with friends so that everyone can use them.

CHAPTER 3

Blockchain Implementation

Gateway to abstractions, by D. Bozhinovski

© Boro Sitnikovski 2021

B. Sitnikovski, *Introducing Blockchain with Lisp*, https://doi.org/10.1007/978-1-4842-6969-5_3

Now that we have equipped ourselves with the ability to write computer programs, we will implement the components (data structures and operations) of the blockchain. Throughout this chapter, we will be using some new procedures. For some of them, we will give a brief explanation. For others, if you are curious, you can get additional details from Racket's manuals.

Every section in this chapter is hands-on, meaning that you will have to implement it as we go through. Exercises are provided to make sure you understand how the procedures we build will be used. Before we start, recall that at the top of every file you have to prepend #lang racket, as we mentioned in the previous chapter.

As before, code snippets that start with a > are to be evaluated in the REPL. Don't save their definitions in the actual target file.

We start by defining serialization. We will rely on it heavily in the next chapter, when peers will send information to each other. Think of it as a neat way to transform data structures to some object that's easy to transfer between peers.

---

❶ Definition 3-1

Serialization is the process of converting an object into a stream of bytes to store the object or transmit it to memory, a database, or a file. **Deserialization** is the opposite process—converting a stream of bytes into an object.

3.1 The wallet.rkt File

In this section, we will implement wallets. They will be used by transactions later to determine the source and the destination of sending/receiving money.

As we discussed earlier, a wallet is a structure that contains a public and a private key. Wallets have this form:

```
1   (struct wallet
2       (private-key public-key)
3       #:prefab)
```

The #: operator represents an **optional keyword argument**—it's basically an argument whose value can be set by referring to this argument's name. In contrast, for ordinary arguments, we have to rely on their order to set their values. For example, in (lambda (x y z) ...), we have to pass values for x and y before we can pass a value for z.

The #:prefab part is new. A prefab ("previously fabricated") structure type is a built-in type that is known to the Racket printer. We can print/display the structure and all of its contents. In addition, we can serialize/deserialize these kinds of structures.

ℹ Definition 3-2

RSA is an asymmetric-key algorithm used to encrypt and decrypt messages, similar in nature to the one described in Section 1.2.2.

We will make a procedure that creates a wallet by generating random public and private keys, and it will rely on the RSA algorithm.

```
1   (define (make-wallet)
2       (letrec ([rsa-impl (get-pk 'rsa libcrypto-factory)]
```

```
3                [privkey (generate-private-key rsa-impl
                 '((nbits 512)))]
4                [pubkey (pk-key->public-only-key privkey)])
5          (wallet (bytes->hex-string
6                    (pk-key->datum privkey 'PrivateKeyInfo))
7                  (bytes->hex-string
8                    (pk-key->datum pubkey 'SubjectPublic
                     KeyInfo)))))
```

All of the procedures we're using come from the crypto package:

- get-pk returns the RSA implementation algorithm.

- generate-private-key generates a private key given algorithm (in this case, RSA).

- pk-key->public-only-key returns a public key given public/private key.

- pk-key->datum returns a public/private key so that it is easily serializable by the next procedure in this list.

- bytes->hex-string converts a hex string (think numbers for example) to bytes, e.g. "0102030304" -> "Hello".

We need to require the necessary packages:

```
1   (require crypto)
2   (require crypto/all)
```

And we export everything so that this procedure can be used as a package.

```
1   (provide (struct-out wallet) make-wallet)
```

The struct-out syntax is exporting the struct together with the procedures it generates.

Here's an example of a generated wallet:

```
1   > (make-wallet)
2   '#s(wallet
3       "3082015502010030..."
4       "305c300d06092a86...")
```

We now have a way to create wallets for our blockchain.

✎ Exercise 3-1

Create a wallet using make-wallet and store it in a variable using define.

✎ Exercise 3-2

Extract the private and the public key of the previously created wallet. The code should look something like (wallet-?? (make-wallet)).

✎ Exercise 3-3

Get yourself briefly introduced to the procedures used in the crypto package by reading the manuals.

Hint: If your local documentation does not contain information about the crypto package, refer to https://docs.racket-lang.org.

3.2 The block.rkt File

Recall that a blockchain is simply a list of blocks, as depicted in Figure 1-4 (Chapter 1). Thus, a block is the building block of a blockchain, and in this section, we will provide an implementation of blocks.

3.2.1 Construction

A block should contain the current hash, the previous hash, the data, and the timestamp that it was generated:

```
1   > (struct block
2     (current-hash previous-hash data timestamp)
3     #:prefab)
```

Using a hashing algorithm will allow us to confirm that the block is valid.

In general, blocks can contain any data, not just transactions, but we are limiting them to transactions for now. We will also add a nonce field for the Hashcash algorithm. We will see the purpose of this field in a moment:

```
1   (struct block
2     (current-hash previous-hash transaction timestamp nonce)
3     #:prefab)
```

Our block also contains a transaction that is roughly of the following form:

```
1   > (struct transaction
2     (signature from to value)
3     #:prefab)
```

We will implement transactions in details later.

Here's one way to generate a block:

```
1   > (block "123456" "234" (transaction "BoroS" "Boro" "You"
      123) 1 1)
2   '#s(block "123456" "234" #s(transaction "BoroS" "Boro"
      "You" 123)
3   1 1)
```

For example, this block makes a transaction from "Boro" to "You" with the value of 123, and with a timestamp and a nonce of 1.

3.2.2 Hashing and Verification

Next, we will implement a procedure that calculates a block's hash. We will use the SHA hashing algorithm.

ℹ Definition 3-3

SHA is a hashing algorithm that takes an input and produces a hash value.

Here's how the procedure looks:

```
1  (define (calculate-block-hash previous-hash timestamp
       transaction nonce)
2    (bytes->hex-string (sha256 (bytes-append
3           (string->bytes/utf-8 previous-hash)
4           (string->bytes/utf-8 (number->string timestamp))
5           (string->bytes/utf-8 (~a (serialize
               transaction)))
6           (string->bytes/utf-8 (number->string nonce))))))
```

There are a few things to note here:

- We expect every field in the structure to be of type string. This will make things much easier later, e.g., when we want to store the blockchain in a data file.

- If you check the manuals for sha256, you will notice it accepts bytes. That means we have to convert every field to bytes using string->bytes/utf-8 and then append all these bytes together before hashing them.

- number->string converts a number to a string, so for example 3 -> "3" and ~a does the same thing but it can also convert objects to string.

- We use serialize on a transaction. This procedure accepts an object and returns an S-expression containing the same contents. Not all objects can be serialized; however, in this case, we use #:prefab which additionally makes structures serializable.

- Finally, we store the hash as a hex string. Think of hex as a way to store a string from readable characters to numbers, e.g. "Hello" -> "0102030304".

As an example, this is how we calculate the hash of our earlier example block:

```
1  > (calculate-block-hash  "234"  1  (transaction  "BoroS"
       "Boro"  "You"
2  "a book") 1)
3  "5e2889a76a464ea19a493a74d2da991a78626fc1fa9070340c2284
   ad92f4dd17"
```

Now that we have a way to calculate a block's hash, we also need a way to verify it. To do that, we just hash the block's contents again and compare this hash to the one stored in the block:

```
1  (define (valid-block? bl)
2    (equal? (block-current-hash bl)
3            (calculate-block-hash (block-previous-hash bl)
4                                  (block-timestamp bl)
5                                  (block-transaction bl)
6                                  (block-nonce bl))))
```

3.2.3 Hashcash Algorithm

At this point, we have everything we need to implement the Hashcash algorithm.

```
1  (define difficulty 2)
2  (define target (bytes->hex-string (make-bytes difficulty 32)))
```

We set the difficulty to 2, and thus the target will contain a difficulty number of bytes using the built-in procedure called make-bytes.

A block will be considered mined if the hash matches the target, given the difficulty:

```
1  (define (mined-block? block-hash)
2    (equal? (subbytes (hex-string->bytes block-hash) 1
       difficulty)
3            (subbytes (hex-string->bytes target) 1
             difficulty)))
```

A couple of things to note here:

- hex-string->bytes is just a way to convert a hex string, e.g. "0102030304" -> #"\1\2\3\3\4".

- subbytes takes a list of bytes, a start, and an end point and returns that sublist.

- Thus, given a random hash, we consider it to be valid if its first two (in this case, per difficulty) bytes match the target.

The actual Hashcash procedure is as follows:

```
1  (define (make-and-mine-block
2             previous-hash timestamp transaction nonce)
3    (let ([current-hash (calculate-block-hash
```

```
4                        previous-hash timestamp transaction nonce)])
5        (if (mined-block? current-hash)
6            (block current-hash previous-hash transaction
             timestamp nonce)
7            (make-and-mine-block
8             previous-hash timestamp transaction
              (+ nonce 1)))))
```

This procedure keeps increasing the nonce until a block is valid, at which point it is returned. That is, we continuously change the nonce until sha256 produces a hash that matches the target. This defines the foundations of mining (proof of work).

For example, here's how we can mine the earlier block we gave as an example:

```
1   > (define mined-block (make-and-mine-block "234" 1
      (transaction "BoroS"
2     "Boro" "You" "a book") 1))
3   > (block-nonce mined-block)
4   337
5   > (block-previous-hash mined-block)
6   "234"
7   > (block-current-hash mined-block)
8   "e920d627196658b64e349c1d3d6f2de1ab308d98d1c48130ee36df47
      ef25ee9a"
```

Note that nonce had to go up to 337 for the mining conditionals to be fulfilled. This is the amount of "work" that was required. In some cases, it will be smaller, and in others, it will be larger.

Lastly, we need a small helper procedure:

```
1   (define (mine-block transaction previous-hash)
2     (make-and-mine-block
3      previous-hash (current-milliseconds) transaction 1))
```

current-milliseconds returns the current time in milliseconds since midnight UTC, January 1, 1970.

We provide these structures and procedures:

```
1   (provide (struct-out block) mine-block valid-block? mined-
    block?)
```

And make sure we require all the necessary packages:

```
1   (require (only-in file/sha1 hex-string->bytes))
2   (require (only-in sha sha256))
3   (require (only-in sha bytes->hex-string))
4   (require racket/serialize)
```

The only-in syntax imports only specific objects from a package that we specify, instead of importing everything.

At this point, besides being able to create and sign wallets, we now also have the necessary procedures to create and mine a block.

✏ Exercise 3-4

Create a block (with a transaction) using block (and transaction) and store it in a variable using define. Then, calculate its hash using calculate-block-hash.

✏ Exercise 3-5

Use make-and-mine-block on a block you generated. What's the nonce count, i.e., how much "work" (processing) did it take to mine that block?

✏ Exercise 3-6

Use valid-block? on the block in the previous exercise. Now use valid-block? on that block where its nonce is 1.

Hint: To generate a "new" block out of an existing one called bl, you can use:

```
1    (block (block-current-hash bl)
2            (block-previous-hash bl)
3            (block-transaction bl)
4            (block-timestamp bl)
5            (block-nonce bl))
```

3.3 The utils.rkt File

This file will contain common procedures that will be used by other components.

A procedure that we will use often is true-for-all?. It returns true if a predicate satisfies all members of the list, and false otherwise:

```
1    (define (true-for-all? pred list)
2      (cond
3        [(empty? list) #t]
4        [(pred (car list)) (true-for-all? pred (cdr list))]
5        [else #f]))
```

Here's an example how we can use it:

```
1   > (true-for-all? (lambda (x) (> x 3)) '(1 2 3))
2   #f
3   > (true-for-all? (lambda (x) (> x 3)) '(4 5 6))
4   #t
```

Next, we'll have a need for a procedure to export a struct into a file:

```
1   (define (struct->file object file)
2     (let ([out (open-output-file file #:exists 'replace)])
3       (write (serialize object) out)
4       (close-output-port out)))
```

open-output-file returns an object in memory, which we can then write to using write. When we do that, it will write to the opened file. close-output-port closes this object in memory. This procedure will serialize a struct and then will write the serialized contents to a file.

The following procedure is the opposite of struct->file: given a file, it will return a struct by opening the file, reading its contents, and deserializing its contents.

```
1   (define (file->struct file)
2     (letrec ([in (open-input-file file)]
3              [result (read in)])
4       (close-input-port in)
5       (deserialize result)))
```

A few notes here:

- read will read and return data from in (the opposite of write).

- open-input-file is similar to open-output-file, except that it is used to read from a file using read.

- deserialize is the opposite of serialize.

We provide these procedures:

```
1    (provide true-for-all? struct->file file->struct)
```

And make sure we require all the necessary packages:

```
1    (require racket/serialize)
```

Now we have a way to write our blockchain data into the filesystem (and read it from the filesystem). This way, our blockchain data can persist.

✏ Exercise 3-7

Use `struct->file` on some block to store it in a file. Then, use `file->struct` on that same file. Did you get the same block? Next, use a text editor to open the file you created. What do the file contents look like?

3.4 Transactions

In this section, we will implement the procedures for signing and verifying transactions, as depicted in Figure 1-2 (Chapter 1).

3.4.1 The transaction-io.rkt File

The `transaction` structure will consist of a `transaction-io` structure (transaction input/output). The transaction input will represent the blockchain address from which the money was sent, and the transaction output will represent the blockchain address to which the money was sent.

This structure contains a hash so that we're able to verify its validity. It also has a value, an owner, and a timestamp.

```
1  (struct transaction-io
2    (transaction-hash value owner timestamp)
3    #:prefab)
```

Similarly to a block, we will use the same code for creating a hash and also rely on serialization:

```
1  (define (calculate-transaction-io-hash value owner
      timestamp)
2    (bytes->hex-string (sha256 (bytes-append
3           (string->bytes/utf-8 (number->string value))
4           (string->bytes/utf-8 (~a (serialize owner)))
5           (string->bytes/utf-8 (number->string
              timestamp))))))
```

make-transaction-io is a helper procedure that will initialize timestamp as well:

```
1  (define (make-transaction-io value owner)
2    (let ([timestamp (current-milliseconds)])
3      (transaction-io
4       (calculate-transaction-io-hash value owner timestamp)
5       value
6       owner
7       timestamp)))
```

A transaction-io structure is valid if its hash is equal to the hash of the value, owner, and the timestamp:

```
1  (define (valid-transaction-io? t-in)
2    (equal? (transaction-io-transaction-hash t-in)
3            (calculate-transaction-io-hash
```

```
4                  (transaction-io-value t-in)
5                  (transaction-io-owner t-in)
6                  (transaction-io-timestamp  t-in))))
```

Here's an example usage:

```
1  > (make-transaction-io 123 "Some person")
2  '#s(transaction-io "df652a3c15feba2eb9071cfdd810130c971f7
   fe7494a4710ee62
3  2fca11f0d83e" 123 "Some person" 1573765357289)
4  > (valid-transaction-io? (transaction-io
   "df652a3c15feba2eb9071cfdd81013
5  0c971f7fe7494a4710ee622fca11f0d83e" 123 "Some person"
   1573765357289))
6  #t
7  > (valid-transaction-io? (transaction-io "badhash" 123
   "Some person"
8  1573765357289))
9  #f
```

Finally, we import the necessary packages and export the procedures:

```
1  (require (only-in sha sha256))
2  (require (only-in sha bytes->hex-string))
3  (require racket/serialize)
4
5  (provide (struct-out transaction-io)
6           make-transaction-io valid-transaction-io?)
```

Now that we have a way to store transaction inputs/outputs, we can proceed with the actual transaction implementation.

3.4.2 The transaction.rkt File

This file will contain procedures for signing and verifying transactions. It will also use transaction inputs and outputs and store them in a single transaction.

Here's everything that we will need to require:

```
1  (require "transaction-io.rkt")
2  (require "utils.rkt")
3  (require (only-in file/sha1 hex-string->bytes))
4  (require "wallet.rkt")
5  (require crypto)
6  (require crypto/all)
7  (require racket/serialize)
```

A transaction contains a signature, sender, receiver, value, and a list of inputs and outputs (transaction-io objects).

```
1  (struct transaction
2    (signature from to value inputs outputs)
3    #:prefab)
```

ⓘ Definition 3-4

In Racket, a **crypto factory** consists of specific implementations of crypto-graphic algorithms.

In addition to the code, we need to use all crypto factories. They will allow us to use some procedures, for example hex<->pk-key:

```
1  (use-all-factories!)
```

We will need a procedure that makes an empty, unsigned, and unprocessed (no input outputs) transaction. This procedure will be used later when we send money or create the first (genesis) transaction.

```
1  (define (make-transaction from to value inputs)
2    (transaction
3      ""
4      from
5      to
6      value
7      inputs
8      '()))
```

3.4.2.1 Digital Signatures

Next, we need a procedure to sign a transaction. It is similar to the procedures we wrote earlier where we used hashing, in that we get all bytes from the structure and append them. The difference, in this case, is that we will be using digital signatures for signing and verifying data.

To create a digital signature, we use a hashing procedure (in this case, it is using the SHA algorithm). The private key is then used to encrypt the produced hash. The encrypted hash will represent the digital signature.

```
1  (define (sign-transaction from to value)
2    (let ([privkey (wallet-private-key from)]
3          [pubkey (wallet-public-key from)])
4      (bytes->hex-string
5        (digest/sign
```

```
6        (datum->pk-key (hex-string->bytes privkey)
          'PrivateKeyInfo)
7        'sha1
8        (bytes-append
9         (string->bytes/utf-8 (~a (serialize from)))
10        (string->bytes/utf-8 (~a (serialize to)))
11        (string->bytes/utf-8 (number->string value)))))))))
```

digest/sign is the procedure that does the hashing and encryption. It accepts a private key, an algorithm,[1] and bytes, and it returns encrypted data.

3.4.2.2 Processing Transactions

Next, we implement a procedure for processing transactions which will:

- Sum all the inputs within inputs-sum.

- Calculate the leftover, which is the difference between inputs-sum and the current transaction's value.

- Generate new outputs based on the transaction's value and leftover.

- Combine the old outputs (outputs) and new outputs (new-outputs) to the newly generated transaction (inputs remain unchanged and will be used by the UTXO implementation later).

- Use foldr + 0 l to calculate the sum of a list of numbers, l.

---

[1]In this case, this is a quoted expression ('sha1) but the algorithm itself is implemented in the crypto factories.

In other words, based on some transaction inputs, the procedure will create transaction outputs that contain the transaction's value and leftover money:

```
1    (define (process-transaction t)
2      (letrec
3          ([inputs (transaction-inputs t)]
4           [outputs (transaction-outputs t)]
5           [value (transaction-value t)]
6           [inputs-sum
7            (foldr + 0 (map (lambda (i) (transaction-io-value
             i)) inputs))]
8           [leftover (- inputs-sum value)]
9           [new-outputs
10           (list
11            (make-transaction-io value (transaction-to t))
12            (make-transaction-io leftover (transaction-from
             t)))])
13        (transaction
14         (sign-transaction (transaction-from t)
15                           (transaction-to t)
16                           (transaction-value t))
17         (transaction-from t)
18         (transaction-to t)
19         value
20         inputs
21         (append new-outputs outputs)))))
```

We will also need a procedure that checks a transaction signature:

```
1    (define (valid-transaction-signature? t)
2      (let ([pubkey (wallet-public-key (transaction-from t))])
3        (digest/verify
```

```
4       (datum->pk-key (hex-string->bytes pubkey)
        'SubjectPublicKeyInfo)
5       'sha1
6       (bytes-append
7        (string->bytes/utf-8 (~a (serialize
         (transaction-from t))))
8        (string->bytes/utf-8 (~a (serialize
         (transaction-to t))))
9        (string->bytes/utf-8 (number->string
         (transaction-value t))))
10       (hex-string->bytes (transaction-signature t)))))
```

digest/verify is the opposite of digest/sign, in that instead of signing, it determines if a signature is valid.

Lastly, we will need a procedure that determines transaction validity under the following conditions:

- Its signature is valid: valid-transaction-signature?

- All outputs are valid: valid-transaction-io?

- The sum of the inputs is greater than or equal to the sum of the outputs: >= sum-inputs sum-outputs. This resolves the problem of double-spending.

```
1   (define (valid-transaction? t)
2     (let ([sum-inputs
3            (foldr + 0 (map (lambda (t) (transaction-io-
            value t))
4                             (transaction-inputs t)))]
5           [sum-outputs
6            (foldr + 0 (map (lambda (t) (transaction-io-
            value t))
7                             (transaction-outputs t)))])
```

```
8        (and
9          (valid-transaction-signature? t)
10         (true-for-all? valid-transaction-io? (transaction-
           outputs t))
11         (>= sum-inputs sum-outputs))))
```

The (and ...) syntax will return #t if all values passed to it are #t, and it will return #f otherwise. In contrast, (or ...) will return #t if at least one value passed to it is #t, and #f otherwise.

Finally, we export the following:

```
1   (provide (all-from-out "transaction-io.rkt")
2            (struct-out transaction)
3            make-transaction process-transaction valid-
             transaction?)
```

The all-from-out syntax specifies all objects that we import (and that are exported) from the target. In this case, besides the file exporting the transaction structure with a couple of procedures, it also exports everything from transaction-io.rkt.

In addition to wallets and blocks, our implementation also supports the creation and processing of transactions.

✐ Exercise 3-8

Create a transaction, process it, and verify it using the procedures above.

Hint: Use make-transaction, process-transaction, and valid-transaction?, respectively.

3.5 The blockchain.rkt File

We will now implement the final component—the blockchain. We'll need to require a bunch of stuff:

```
1  (require "block.rkt")
2  (require "transaction.rkt")
3  (require "utils.rkt")
4  (require "wallet.rkt")
```

Recall that UTXO is just a list of transaction-io objects, where it represents unspent transaction outputs. In a way, it resembles the initial balance of wallets. Thus, the structure will contain a list of blocks and UTXO:

```
1  (struct blockchain
2    (blocks utxo)
3    #:prefab)
```

3.5.1 Initialization

We will need a procedure for the initialization of the blockchain. It should accept the genesis transaction, genesis hash, and UTXO:

```
1  (define (init-blockchain t seed-hash utxo)
2    (blockchain (cons (mine-block (process-transaction t)
     seed-hash) '())
3                utxo))
```

One way to initialize a blockchain is as follows:

```
1  > (define coin-base (make-wallet))
2  > (define wallet-a (make-wallet))
3  > (define genesis-t (make-transaction coin-base wallet-a
     100  '()))
4  > (define utxo (list
```

```
5  >                   (make-transaction-io 100 wallet-a)))
6  > (define blockchain (init-blockchain genesis-t
     "1337cafe"  utxo))
```

3.5.2 Rewards

In the original Bitcoin implementation, the block reward starts at 50 coins for the first block and halves on every 210000 blocks. This means that every block up until block 210000 will reward 50 coins, while block 210001 will reward 25. In other words, the reward is calculated using the following formula, where b is the number of blocks.

$$\frac{2^{\frac{b}{210000}}}{50}$$

We follow the same algorithm. We start with 50 coins initially and halve them on every 210000 blocks.

```
1  (define (mining-reward-factor blocks)
2    (/ 50 (expt 2 (floor (/ (length blocks) 210000)))))
```

3.5.3 Adding a Transaction

The next procedure will add a transaction to the blockchain. It should:

1. Mine a block.

2. Create a new UTXO based on the processed transaction outputs, inputs, and the current UTXO.

3. Generate a new list of blocks by adding the newly mined block.

4. Calculate the rewards based on the current UTXO.

Additionally, UTXO will be treated as a set so that we can easily remove specific inputs and append new transactions using set operations.

```
1    (define (add-transaction-to-blockchain b t)
2      (letrec ([hashed-blockchain
3                 (mine-block t
4                   (block-current-hash (car (blockchain-blocks
                       b)))))]
5                [processed-inputs (transaction-inputs t)]
6                [processed-outputs (transaction-outputs t)]
7                [utxo (set-union processed-outputs
8                                  (set-subtract (blockchain-
                                   utxo b)
9                                                 processed-
                                                  inputs))]
10               [new-blocks (cons hashed-blockchain
                  (blockchain-blocks b))]
11               [utxo-rewarded (cons
12                                (make-transaction-io
13                                 (mining-reward-factor new-
                                   blocks)
14                                 (transaction-from t))
15                                utxo)])
16        (blockchain
17         new-blocks
18         utxo-rewarded)))
```

There is another thing about add-transaction-to-blockchain: given a blockchain and a transaction, it returns a new, updated blockchain. This newly returned blockchain will be the latest that should be used, since the previous one will not contain this new transaction. This way, we avoid mutating the previous blockchain.

Next, we will create a procedure that will determine the balance of a wallet—the sum of all unspent transactions for the matching owner:

```
1   (define (balance-wallet-blockchain  b   w)
2     (letrec ([utxo (blockchain-utxo b)]
3             [my-ts (filter
4                         (lambda (t) (equal? w (transaction-io-
                          owner t)))
5                         utxo)])
6       (foldr + 0 (map (lambda (t) (transaction-io-value t))
        my-ts))))
```

We will also need a procedure that will send money from one wallet to another by initiating a transaction and then adding it to the blockchain for processing. my-ts will contain the current receiver's transaction inputs. Finally, we add the transaction to the blockchain only if it is valid.

```
1   (define (send-money-blockchain b from to value)
2     (letrec ([my-ts
3                 (filter (lambda (t) (equal? from (transaction-
                  io-owner t)))
4                         (blockchain-utxo b))]
5               [t (make-transaction from to value my-ts)])
6       (if (transaction? t)
7           (let ([processed-transaction (process-transaction t)])
8             (if (and
9                   (>= (balance-wallet-blockchain b from)
                      value)
10                  (valid-transaction? processed-transaction))
11                (add-transaction-to-blockchain b processed-
                  transaction)
12                b))
13            (add-transaction-to-blockchain b '()))))
```

3.5.4 Verification

We will now introduce a procedure that determines blockchain validity under the following conditions:

- All blocks are valid using valid-block?.

- Previous hashes are matching using the equal? check by comparing the previous hash of all blocks (except the last) to the current hash of all blocks (except the first).

- All transactions are valid using valid-transaction?.

- All blocks are mined using mined-block?.

```
1   (define (valid-blockchain? b)
2     (let ([blocks (blockchain-blocks b)])
3       (and
4        (true-for-all? valid-block? blocks)
5        (equal? (drop-right (map block-previous-hash
           blocks) 1)
6                (cdr (map block-current-hash blocks)))
7        (true-for-all?
8         valid-transaction? (map
9                             (lambda (block) (block-
                              transaction block))
10                            blocks))
11        (true-for-all?
12         mined-block? (map block-current-hash blocks)))))
```

Finally, we export everything:

```
1   (provide (all-from-out "block.rkt")
2             (all-from-out "transaction.rkt")
3             (all-from-out "wallet.rkt")
4             (struct-out blockchain)
5             init-blockchain send-money-blockchain
6             balance-wallet-blockchain valid-blockchain?)
```

We now have all the necessary components: managing wallets, blocks, transactions, and finally the blockchain.

✏ Exercise 3-9

Create two sets and use set-subtract, set-union, and set-intersect on them. Observe the results.

✏ Exercise 3-10

Initialize a blockchain with init-blockchain and add a transaction to it using add-transaction-to-blockchain.

✏ Exercise 3-11

Use valid-blockchain? on the blockchain in the previous exercise (do this before adding the new transaction, and again after adding the new transaction).

✏ Exercise 3-12

Make a transfer in a blockchain using send-money-blockchain.

3.6 Integrating Components

In this section, we will combine all the various parts into a single point and show how they can be easily used.

3.6.1 The main-helper.rkt File

This file will import everything from blockchain.rkt and utils.rkt and will provide some printing procedures.

```
1  (require "blockchain.rkt")
2  (require "utils.rkt")
```

The next procedure will convert a transaction object to a printable string. It will use substring to only print a subset of the hash (since it may be too big), and it will also use format, which is a string-formatting procedure that replaces every ~a in a string with the passed argument in order.

```
1  (define (format-transaction t)
2    (format "...~a... sends ...~a... an amount of ~a."
3            (substring (wallet-public-key (transaction-
             from t)) 64 80)
4            (substring (wallet-public-key (transaction-
             to  t)) 64  80)
5            (transaction-value t)))
```

The next procedure will print the details of a block. printf is similar to print, except that it can be used like format:

```
1  (define (print-block bl)
2    (printf "Block information\n=================
3  Hash:\t~a\nHash_p:\t~a\nStamp:\t~a\nNonce:\t~a\nData:
   \t~a\n"
```

```
4        (block-current-hash bl)
5        (block-previous-hash bl)
6        (block-timestamp bl)
7        (block-nonce bl)
8        (format-transaction (block-transaction bl))))
```

Besides using recursion explicitly, there is a built-in for syntax that also allows repetitive computations. To print a blockchain, we will use the for syntax to go through all blocks, print them to the standard output, and then use newline to add a newline character to make the separation of every block obvious:

```
1    (define (print-blockchain b)
2      (for ([block (blockchain-blocks b)])
3        (print-block block)
4        (newline)))
```

We print wallets similarly:

```
1    (define (print-wallets b wallet-a wallet-b)
2      (printf "\nWallet A balance: ~a\nWallet B balance:
       ~a\n\n"
3               (balance-wallet-blockchain b wallet-a)
4               (balance-wallet-blockchain b wallet-b)))
```

And export the procedures:

```
1    (provide (all-from-out "blockchain.rkt")
2             (all-from-out "utils.rkt")
3             format-transaction print-block print-blockchain
             print-wallets)
```

✏ **Exercise 3-13**

Create a transaction and use `format-transaction` to see what it outputs. Repeat the same for a block (`print-block`), blockchain (`print-blockchain`), and wallets (`print-wallets`).

3.6.2 The main.rkt File

This is where we will put all the components together and use them. We start by checking if the blockchain.data file exists by using file-exists?. This file will contain contents from a previous blockchain if it exists. If it doesn't, we will just create a fresh blockchain.

```
1   (require "main-helper.rkt")
2
3   (when (file-exists? "blockchain.data")
4     (begin
4       (printf "Found 'blockchain.data', reading...\n")
6       (print-blockchain (file->struct "blockchain.data"))
7       (exit)))
```

We used when, which is similar to if, except that the else branch is omitted.

Next, we initialize wallets:

```
1   (define coin-base (make-wallet))
2   (define wallet-a (make-wallet))
3   (define wallet-b (make-wallet))
```

We initialize transactions by creating the genesis transaction:

```
1  (printf "Making genesis transaction...\n")
2  (define genesis-t (make-transaction coin-base wallet-a
   100 '()))
```

We initialize the unspent transactions—the genesis transaction:

```
1  (define utxo (list
2                  (make-transaction-io 100 wallet-a)))
```

Finally, we initiate the blockchain by mining the genesis transaction:

```
1  (printf "Mining genesis block...\n")
2  (define blockchain (init-blockchain genesis-t "1337cafe"
   utxo))
3  (print-wallets blockchain wallet-a wallet-b)
```

Making a second transaction:

```
1  (printf "Mining second transaction...\n")
2  (set! blockchain (send-money-blockchain blockchain wallet-a
   wallet-b 2))
3  (print-wallets blockchain wallet-a wallet-b)
```

Making a third transaction:

```
1  (printf "Mining third transaction...\n")
2  (set! blockchain (send-money-blockchain blockchain wallet-b
   wallet-a 1))
3  (print-wallets blockchain wallet-a wallet-b)
```

Attempting to make a fourth transaction:

```
1   (printf "Attempting to mine fourth (not-valid)
    transaction...\n")
2   (set! blockchain (send-money-blockchain blockchain wallet-b
    wallet-a 3))
3   (print-wallets blockchain wallet-a wallet-b)
```

Checking blockchain validity:

```
1   (printf "Blockchain is valid: ~a\n\n" (valid-blockchain?
    blockchain))
```

Printing every block from the blockchain:

```
1   (for ([block (blockchain-blocks blockchain)])
2     (print-block block)
3     (newline))
```

And exporting the blockchain to blockchain.data, which can be reused later.

```
1   (struct->file blockchain "blockchain.data")
2   (printf "Exported blockchain to 'blockchain.data'...\n")
```

Once we create main.rkt, we run it from the Racket > Run menu. It should show the following output:

```
1   Making genesis transaction...
2   Mining genesis block...
3
4   Wallet A balance: 100
5   Wallet B balance: 0
6
7   Mining second transaction...
8
```

```
 9   Wallet A balance: 130
10   Wallet B balance: 20
11
12   Mining third transaction...
13
14   Wallet A balance: 140
15   Wallet B balance: 60
16
17   Attempting to mine fourth (not-valid) transaction...
18
19   Wallet A balance: 140
20   Wallet B balance: 60
21
22   Blockchain is valid: #t
23
24   Block information
25   =================
26   Hash:    e720bb198279a76057280bdf8eb667fe1883d0ae263c5d5d1
                be08697a2f534d1
27   Hash_p: 38200563c1f807be2a5d10ec42dd53acae1f6f804b4c9301
                6b87c974817f065d
28   Stamp:   1529923610574
29   Nonce:   216
30   Data:    ...bb6... sends ...896... an amount of 10.
31
32   Block information
33   =================
34   Hash:    38200563c1f807be2a5d10ec42dd53acae1f6f804b4c93016b
                87c974817f065d
35   Hash_p: 6a20fbe4038bb3b83090e7f767bb24af5164218bba5c751a18
                58262df2a2a847
```

```
36    Stamp:   1529923610405
37    Nonce:   752
38    Data:    ...896... sends ...bb6... an amount of 20.
39
40    Block  information
41    ==================
42    Hash:    6a20fbe4038bb3b83090e7f767bb24af5164218bba5c
               751a1858262df2a2a847
43    Hash_p:  7365656467656e65736973
44    Stamp:   1529923610332
45    Nonce:   220
46    Data:    ...58d... sends ...896... an amount of 100.
47
48    Exported blockchain to 'blockchain.data'...
```

3.7 Summary

We built every component one by one, gradually. Some components are *orthogonal*—they are independent of one another. For example, the wallet implementation does not call any procedures from block, and a block can be used independently of a wallet. When we combine all of the components, we get a blockchain system.

This design allows us to easily extend our system. In the next chapter, we will extend the system with peer-to-peer and smart contracts functionalities without having to change the basic components.

CHAPTER 4

Extending the Blockchain

Extensions, by D. Bozhinovski

© Boro Sitnikovski 2021
B. Sitnikovski, *Introducing Blockchain with Lisp*, https://doi.org/10.1007/978-1-4842-6969-5_4

In the previous chapter, we implemented blockchain's basic components. In this chapter, we will extend the blockchain with smart contracts and peer-to-peer support.

4.1 Smart Contracts Implementation

Bitcoin's blockchain is programmable, which means that the transaction conditions themselves can be programmed by users. For example, users can write *scripts* (short pieces of code) to add requirements that must be satisfied before making a transaction.

In Section 2.4, we created an executable that we can send to our friends, but they cannot change the executable because they don't have the original code. And even if they did have the original code, not all users have programming skills.

The point of smart contracts is to allow non-programmers to adjust the behavior of the transactional process without having to change the original code.

4.1.1 The smart-contracts.rkt File

The idea is to implement a small language, which users can consume. Our implementation will depend on transactions:

```
1  (require "transaction.rkt")
```

We have to extend the original valid-transaction? so that it will also consider contracts when calculating validity:

```
1  (define (valid-transaction-contract? t c)
2    (and (eval-contract t c)
3         (valid-transaction? t)))
```

We will now implement a procedure that will accept a transaction, a contract, a scripting language (which is really just an S-expression), and return some value. The returned value can be true, false, a number, or a string.

```
1    (define (eval-contract t c)
2      (match c
3        [(? number? x) x]
4        [(? string? x) x]
5        [`() #t]
6        [`true #t]
7        [`false #f]
8        [`(if ,co ,tr ,fa) (if co tr fa)]
9        [`(+ ,l ,r) (+ l r)]
10       [else #f]))
```

We used new syntax here, called match. It is similar to cond, except that it can directly compare the structure of an object. For example, ? <expr> <pat> matches when <expr> is true and stores the value in <pat>. In the previous code, if we pass a number, it will return that same number. Additionally, if we pass the value true (i.e., c matches true), then it will return #t. Another example is if c matches a structure of the form (if X Y Z) (quoted[1]), then it will return the evaluation of (if X Y Z).

Here are a few example uses:

```
1    > (define test-transaction (transaction "BoroS" "Boro"
"You" "a book"
2       '() '()))
3    > (eval-contract test-transaction 123)
4    123
```

---

[1]A backtick is like a quote, and a comma is like an "unquote." This is further explained in Appendix A.

```
5    > (eval-contract test-transaction "Hi")
6    "Hi"
7    > (eval-contract test-transaction '())
8    #t
9    > (eval-contract test-transaction 'true)
10   #t
11   > (eval-contract test-transaction 'false)
12   #f
13   > (eval-contract test-transaction '(if #t "Hi" "Hey"))
14   "Hi"
15   > (eval-contract test-transaction '(if #f "Hi" "Hey"))
16   "Hey"
17   > (eval-contract test-transaction '(+ 1 2))
18   3
```

However, we still haven't used any of the transaction's values in our language. Let's extend it with a few more commands:

```
1    ...
2          [`from (transaction-from t)]
3          [`to (transaction-to t)]
4          [`value (transaction-value t)]
5    ...
```

Now we can do something like this:

```
1    > (eval-contract test-transaction 'from)
2    "Boro"
3    > (eval-contract test-transaction 'to)
4    "You"
5    > (eval-contract test-transaction 'value)
6    "a book"
```

We will implement a few more operators so that the scripting language becomes more expressive:

```
1    ...
2        [`(* ,l ,r) (* l r)]
3        [`(- ,l ,r) (- l r)]
4        [`(= ,l ,r) (equal? l r)]
5        [`(> ,l ,r) (> l r)]
6        [`(< ,l ,r) (< l r)]
7        [`(and ,l ,r) (and l r)]
8        [`(or ,l ,r) (or l r)]
9    ...
```

However, there is a problem in the language implementation. Consider the evaluations of (+ 1 2) and (+ (+ 1 2) 3):

```
1    > (eval-contract test-transaction '(+ 1 2))
2    3
3    > (eval-contract test-transaction '(+ (+ 1 2) 3))
4    . . +: contract violation
```

The problem happens in the matching clause [`(+ ,l ,r) (+ l r)]. When we match against '(+ (+ 1 2) 3)), we end up with (+ '(+ 1 2) 3), and Racket cannot sum a quoted list with a number. The solution to this problem is to *recursively* evaluate every subexpression. So the match turns from [`(+ ,l ,r) (+ l r)] to [`(+ ,l ,r) (+ (eval-contract t l) (eval-contract t r))].

In this case, the evaluation will happen as follows:

```
1    (eval-contract t '(+ (+ 1 2) 3))
2    = (eval-contract t (list '+ (eval-contract t '(+ 1 2))
3                                (eval-contract t 3)))
4    = (eval-contract t (list '+ (+ 1 2) 3))
5    = (eval-contract t (list '+ 3 3))
```

```
6   = (eval-contract t '(+ 3 3))
7   = (eval-contract t 6)
8   = 6
```

It is important to remember the distinction between a quoted list and a non-quoted one; the latter will attempt evaluation. In this case, we juggled the quotations to produce the desired results.

We will have to rewrite all of the operators:

```
1    ...
2         [`(+ ,l ,r) (+ (eval-contract t l) (eval-contract t r))]
3         [`(* ,l ,r) (* (eval-contract t l) (eval-contract t r))]
4         [`(- ,l ,r) (- (eval-contract t l) (eval-contract t r))]
5         [`(= ,l ,r) (= (eval-contract t l) (eval-contract t r))]
6         [`(> ,l ,r) (> (eval-contract t l) (eval-contract t r))]
7         [`(< ,l ,r) (< (eval-contract t l) (eval-contract t r))]
8         [`(and ,l ,r) (and (eval-contract t l) (eval-contract t r))]
9         [`(or ,l ,r) (or (eval-contract t l) (eval-contract t r))]
10   ...
```

The if implementation in the language has the same problem. So we will also change it:

```
1    ...
2         [`(if ,co ,tr ,fa) (if (eval-contract t co)
3                                (eval-contract t tr)
4                                (eval-contract t fa))]
5    ...
```

Thus, the final procedure becomes:

```
1    (define (eval-contract t c)
2      (match c
3        [(? number? x) x]
```

```
4        [(? string? x) x]
5        [`() #t]
6        [`true #t]
7        [`false #f]
8        [`(if ,co ,tr ,fa) (if (eval-contract t co)
9                                  (eval-contract t tr)
10                                 (eval-contract t fa))]
11       [`(+ ,l ,r) (+ (eval-contract t l) (eval-contract t r))]
12       [`from (transaction-from t)]
13       [`to (transaction-to t)]
14       [`value (transaction-value t)]
15       [`(+ ,l ,r) (+ (eval-contract t l) (eval-contract t r))]
16       [`(* ,l ,r) (* (eval-contract t l) (eval-contract t r))]
17       [`(- ,l ,r) (- (eval-contract t l) (eval-contract t r))]
18       [`(= ,l ,r) (= (eval-contract t l) (eval-contract t r))]
19       [`(> ,l ,r) (> (eval-contract t l) (eval-contract t r))]
20       [`(< ,l ,r) (< (eval-contract t l) (eval-contract t r))]
21       [`(and ,l ,r) (and (eval-contract t l) (eval-contract t r))]
22       [`(or ,l ,r) (or (eval-contract t l) (eval-contract t r))]
23       [else #f]))
```

Users can now supply scripting code, such as (if (= (+ 1 2) 3)
from to):

```
1   > (eval-contract test-transaction '(if (= (+ 1 2) 3) from to))
2   "Boro"
3   > (eval-contract test-transaction '(if (= (+ 1 2) 4) from to))
4   "You"
```

Finally, we provide the output, which is just the transaction validity check:

```
1    (provide valid-transaction-contract?)
```

4.1.2 Updating Existing Code

Now that we have implemented the logic for smart contracts, the next thing we need to address is the front-end—how users can use its functionality. For that matter, we will update the implementation to support contracts by reading from a file. If a file named contract.script exists, we will read and parse it (with read) and then run the code.

We will rewrite the money sending procedure in blockchain.rkt to accept contracts. It's the same procedure except that we use valid-transaction-contract? instead of valid-transaction?.

```
1    (define (send-money-blockchain b from to value c)
2      (letrec ([my-ts
3               (filter (lambda (t) (equal? from (transaction-
                  io-owner t)))
4                    (blockchain-utxo b))]
5               [t (make-transaction from to value my-ts)])
6        (if (transaction? t)
7            (let ([processed-transaction
                  (process-transaction t)])
8              (if (and
9                   (>= (balance-wallet-blockchain b from)
                      value)
10                  (valid-transaction-contract? processed-
                     transaction c))
11                 (add-transaction-to-blockchain b processed-
                     transaction)
```

```
12                       b))
13            (add-transaction-to-blockchain b '()))))
```

Next, we will update utils.rkt to add this helper procedure for reading contracts:

```
1   (define (file->contract file)
2     (with-handlers ([exn:fail? (lambda (exn) '())])
3       (read (open-input-file file))))
```

Here, we used with-handlers, which accepts a procedure that handles the case when something may fail—in this case, read or open-input-file.

Finally, make sure to add file->contract to the list of provides in utils.rkt. Additionally, in main.rkt update every use of send-money-blockchain to additionally send (file->contract "contract.script") as an argument so that the contract processed is the one read from contract.script.

We will also need to update blockchain.rkt and main.rkt because they now rely on a procedure implemented in the smart contracts package. We will add (require "smart-contracts.rkt") to them.

✎ Exercise 4-1

Come up with a few valid expressions and evaluate them using eval-contract.

✎ Exercise 4-2

Repeat the previous exercise, but use the contract.script file.

Hint: This exercise might require you to create an executable.

4.2 Peer-to-Peer Implementation

In Section 3.6.2, we used DrRacket to execute the blockchain implementation. That's okay for testing purposes. However, if we wanted to share that implementation with other users and ask them to execute it, it will be kind of inconvenient because there's no way to share data between different users.

In this section, we will implement peer-to-peer support so that users who are interested in our implementation can join the system/community.

Before we dive into the implementation, Figure 4-1 shows a high overview of the architecture that we will build.

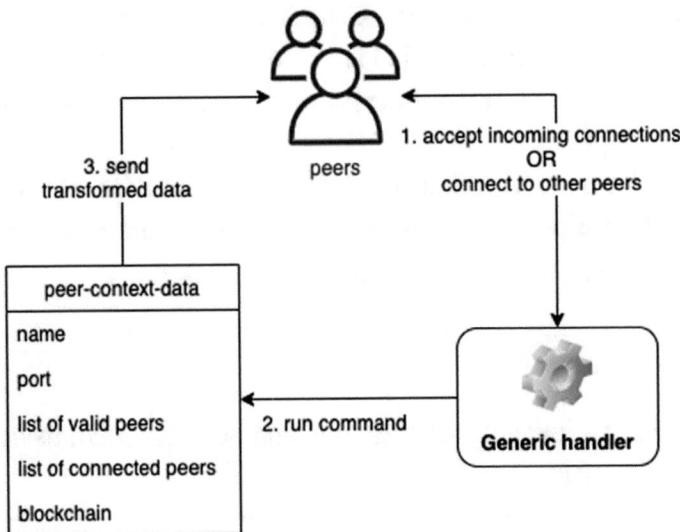

Figure 4-1. *Peer-to-peer architecture*

Every peer node (user connected to the system) list will consist of the following:

- *Peer context data:* Information such as relations with other peers, list of connected peers, and so on.

- *Generic handler:* Transforms the peer context data.

Further, there will be two ways to establish communication with other peers:

- A peer will accept new connections from other peers.

- A peer will try to connect/make new connections to other peers.

Whenever a connection is established, peers will communicate with each other through the generic handler, parsing and evaluating commands such as syncing/updating the blockchain, updating the list of peers, and so on.

Consider this example scenario: Assume there are three peers—Peer 1, Peer 2, and Peer 3. Peer 1 and Peer 2 are online, and Peer 3 is offline at the moment. Peer 1 has the following list of valid peers: (Peer 1, Peer 2, Peer 3). Peer 2's list of peers is empty. According to the diagram, Peer 1 will accept new connections and try to connect to peers. So, Peer 1 will try to connect to Peer 2. This connection will be successful, and the next step is for Peer 1 to send some data to Peer 2 (e.g., the list of valid peers).

Peer 2's list of peers was empty, but now it will be merged with Peer 1, so it will become (Peer 1, Peer 2, Peer 3). Peer 1 and Peer 2 are connected to each other, and they will keep trying to connect to Peer 3. Once Peer 3 becomes available, the same algorithm will be executed and Peer 3 will join the network.

With this approach, the goal is to build a system similar to the high-level description shown in Figures 1-1 and 1-3 (Chapter 1).

Building communication systems of this type is naturally complex. It is suggested you consult the Racket manuals (by pressing the F1 key) for every procedure that you will be using.

4.2.1 The peer-to-peer.rkt File

To start, we will add dependencies for the block implementation and rely on serialization to send data to other peers:

```
1  (require "blockchain.rkt")
2  (require "block.rkt")
3  (require racket/serialize)
```

4.2.1.1 Peer Context Structure

We will implement structures that hold information about the peers so that we have a reference to send data to the correct destinations. The peer-info structure contains an IP address and a port of a peer. Think of an IP address and a port similar to a street address and a number, respectively.

```
1  (struct peer-info
2    (ip port)
3    #:prefab)
```

The peer-info-io structure additionally contains IO ports (think communication channels) for sending and receiving data between peers:

```
1  (struct peer-info-io
2    (peer-info input-port output-port)
3    #:prefab)
```

The reason we separate peer-info and peer-info-io is that later in main-p2p.rkt, we won't have the context of input/output ports (before a connection to a peer is established), so it gives us a nice way to reuse the structure.

Finally, peer-context-data contains all the information needed for a single peer, that is:

- List of valid peers

- List of connected peers

- A reference to the blockchain

```
1  (struct peer-context-data
2    (name
3     port
4     [valid-peers #:mutable]
5     [connected-peers #:mutable]
6     [blockchain #:mutable])
7    #:prefab)
```

The list[2] of valid peers will be updated depending on the information retrieved from the connected peers. The list of connected peers will be a (not necessarily strict) subset of valid-peers. The blockchain will be updated with the data combined from all peers. We make them mutable because it provides an easy way to update the data.

4.2.1.2 Generic Handler

The generic handler will be a handler procedure that will be used both by the server (the "accepting new connections" part of the diagram) and the client (the "connecting to new peers" part of the diagram). It will be a procedure that accepts commands (commands similar in nature to the smart contracts' eval-contract implementation) and then does something depending on the command.

---

[2]More precisely, "the set," since we will use operations such as subtract.

Here's a list of commands that peers will send to each other:

Request	Response	Notes
get-valid-peers	valid-peers:X	A peer may request a list of valid peers. The response will be X – valid peers. Note that this response should automatically trigger the valid-peers command.
get-latest-blockchain	latest-blockchain:X	A peer may request the latest blockchain from another peer. The response will be X - the latest version of the blockchain. This should trigger the latest-blockchain command.
latest-blockchain:X		When a peer gets this request, it will update the blockchain, given it is valid.
valid-peers:X		When a peer gets this request, it will update the list of valid peers.

The commands in this table will allow the peers to sync data with each other. We will now provide the handler implementation. It accepts a peer-context and input/output ports. Given these, it will read the input (command) and send the appropriate output (evaluated command) back to the peer:

```
1   (define (handler peer-context in out)
2     (flush-output out)
3     (define line (read-line in))
4     (when (string? line) ; it can be eof
5       (cond [(string-prefix? line "get-valid-peers")
```

```
 6            (fprintf out "valid-peers:~a\n"
 7                       (serialize
 8                        (set->list
 9                         (peer-context-data-valid-peers peer-
                           context))))
10            (handler peer-context in out)]
11           [(string-prefix? line "get-latest-blockchain")
12            (fprintf out "latest-blockchain:")
13            (write
14             (serialize (peer-context-data-blockchain peer-
                context)) out)
15            (handler peer-context in out)]
16           [(string-prefix? line "latest-blockchain:")
17            (begin (maybe-update-blockchain peer-context
                line)
18                   (handler peer-context in out))]
19           [(string-prefix? line "valid-peers:")
20            (begin (maybe-update-valid-peers peer-context
                line)
21                   (handler peer-context in out))]
22           [(string-prefix? line "exit")
23            (fprintf out "bye\n")]
24           [else (handler peer-context in out)])))
```

We used some new procedures here:

- An output buffer (output communication channel
  with a peer) is usually filled with bytes. We need to
  flush (empty) this buffer every time we want to send a
  message, to avoid resending the previous messages. We
  achieve this using `flush-output`.

- read-line is similar to read except that it will stop
  reading once a newline is reached.

- `string-prefix?` checks to see if a string starts with some other string.

- `fprintf` is similar to `printf` except that we can also supply the first argument to specify where this message should be sent.

- `set->list` converts a set to a list.

There's a little trick involved in the `latest-blockchain` case—we used `write` instead of (`fprintf out "latest-blockchain:~a\n"`). The reason for that is that `print` (and thus `printf` and `fprintf`) cannot be relied on for output that needs to be formatted in a specific way. For example, `print` prints strings with quotation marks (to make the printed data more legible to the user), and this will be messed up when we try to deserialize the data we received, so we want to send the data in its "raw" format.

The next step is to implement procedures for updating the blockchain and the list of valid peers, under the conditions that the blockchain is valid and it has higher effort than ours.

```
1   (define (maybe-update-blockchain peer-context line)
2     (let ([latest-blockchain
3            (trim-helper line #rx"(latest-blockchain:|
            [\r\n]+)")]
4           [current-blockchain
5            (peer-context-data-blockchain peer-context)])
6       (when (and (valid-blockchain? latest-blockchain)
7                  (> (get-blockchain-effort latest-
                   blockchain)
8                     (get-blockchain-effort current-
                     blockchain)))
9         (printf "Blockchain updated for peer ~a\n"
10                (peer-context-data-name peer-context))
```

```
11          (set-peer-context-data-blockchain! peer-context
12                                       latest-
                                         blockchain))))
```

We used #rx"..." for the first time—this specifies a regular expression. Think of it as a way to define a search pattern in some string.

For example, #rx"(latest-blockchain:|[\r\n]+)" matches the following strings:

- latest-blockchain:a\n

- latest-blockchain:b\n

- In general, latest-blockchain:...\n

The previous procedure will update the blockchain only when it is valid and the effort is higher than the current one. We define the effort as the sum of all blocks' nonces:

```
1   (define (get-blockchain-effort b)
2     (foldl + 0 (map block-nonce (blockchain-blocks b))))
```

To update the list of valid peers is to merge the current list of valid peers with the newly received list, thus mutating the peer-context structure:

```
1   (define (maybe-update-valid-peers peer-context line)
2     (let ([valid-peers (list->set
3                         (trim-helper line #rx"(valid-
                          peers:|[\r\n]+)"))]
4           [current-valid-peers (peer-context-data-valid-peers
5                                 peer-context)])
6       (set-peer-context-data-valid-peers!
7        peer-context
8        (set-union current-valid-peers valid-peers))))
```

We also used this procedure, which is just a helper one that will remove a command (prefix) from a string, allowing us to focus on the input. For example, when we receive valid-peers:X, it will remove valid-peers:, allowing us to retrieve X easily.

```
1  (define (trim-helper line x)
2    (deserialize
3     (read
4      (open-input-string
5       (string-replace line x "")))))
```

This concludes the handler implementation. Now there is a procedure that can be used by peers to accept commands and update the list of peers and the blockchain. In the next section, we will implement the communication between the peers—they should communicate with each other using these commands that we implemented.

4.2.1.3 Server Implementation

When a peer connects to another peer (a server), here's what should happen:

1. The server should wait for the incoming peer to send some command.

2. The server should use the handler procedure to handle the necessary data.

3. The server should send the transformed data back to the incoming peer.

However, if more than one peer connects, then the procedure will "block," in the sense that the second peer will have to wait for the first one to be served, the third will have to wait for the second, and so on.

To resolve this issue, we turn to threads. `accept-and-handle` is the main procedure that will serve the incoming peers. The procedure accepts a connection (listener object) and a peer context and launches `handler` in a thread for every incoming connection:

```
1   (define (accept-and-handle listener peer-context)
2     (define-values (in out) (tcp-accept listener))
3     (thread
4       (lambda ()
5         (handler peer-context in out)
6         (close-input-port in)
7         (close-output-port out))))
```

We used a new procedure called `tcp-accept` that accepts a connection and returns the input (to read data) and the output ports (to send data). Using the `define-values` syntax, we store both of these values.

`peers/serve` is the main server listener. This is straight copy-pasted from the Racket documentation, and the curious reader can navigate to the documentation and read more about the implementation details. In short, a *custodian* is a kind of container that ensures there are no bogus threads or input/output ports in the memory and takes care of this for us.

```
1    (define (peers/serve peer-context)
2      (define main-cust (make-custodian))
3      (parameterize ([current-custodian main-cust])
4        (define listener
5          (tcp-listen (peer-context-data-port peer-context)
                        5 #t))
6        (define (loop)
7          (accept-and-handle listener peer-context)
8          (loop))
9        (thread loop))
10     (lambda ()
11       (custodian-shutdown-all main-cust)))
```

The tcp-listen procedure keeps listening to a specific port for new incoming connections.

4.2.1.4 Client Implementation

Next, we will implement connect-and-handle—a procedure that tries to connect to other peers, whereas previously we constructed a procedure that was supposed to serve incoming peers. This procedure will be similar to accept-and-handle, but kind of dual, in that it does not accept new connections. Rather, it tries to make a new connection:

```
1   (define (connect-and-handle peer-context peer)
2     (begin
3       (define-values (in out)
4         (tcp-connect (peer-info-ip peer)
5                      (peer-info-port peer)))
6
7       (define current-peer-io (peer-info-io peer in out))
8
9       (set-peer-context-data-connected-peers!
10       peer-context
11       (cons current-peer-io
12             (peer-context-data-connected-peers peer-
              context)))
13
14       (thread
15        (lambda ()
16          (handler peer-context in out)
17          (close-input-port in)
18          (close-output-port out)
19
20          (set-peer-context-data-connected-peers!
```

```
21            peer-context
22            (set-remove
23             (peer-context-data-connected-peers peer-context)
24             current-peer-io))))))
```

This procedure is quite long so it deserves some unpacking:

1. The tcp-connect procedure tries to make a connection to a specific IP address and port (values that we extract from the peer-info structure).

2. When the connection is successful, tcp-connect will return the input and output ports, which we can use to read data from and write data to, respectively.

3. Next, the specific list of connected peers for the current context will be updated.

4. Finally, we launch a thread, using handler to handle the communication. When the connection is finished, we do a cleanup and remove the peer from the list of peers.

The next procedure is to make sure we're connected with all known peers. We use threads, again, for the same reason as in the server—we do not want this procedure to block the program from connecting to other clients while it tries to connect to one. This procedure is dual to peers/serve, and tcp-connect is dual to tcp-accept. We use sleep to wait for a few seconds before processing again in order to make the process more performant.

```
1   (define (peers/connect peer-context)
2     (define main-cust (make-custodian))
3     (parameterize ([current-custodian main-cust])
4       (define (loop)
```

```
5        (let ([potential-peers (get-potential-peers peer-
         context)])
6          (for ([peer potential-peers])
7            (with-handlers ([exn:fail? (lambda (x) #t)])
8              (connect-and-handle peer-context peer))))
9          (sleep 10)
10         (loop))
11       (thread loop))
12     (lambda ()
13       (custodian-shutdown-all main-cust)))
```

To implement get-potential-peers, we first get the list of connected and valid peers from the peer context. The valid peers that are not in the list of connected peers are potential peers we can make new connections with.

```
1    (define (get-potential-peers peer-context)
2      (let ([current-connected-peers
3             (list->set
4               (map peer-info-io-peer-info
5                    (peer-context-data-connected-peers peer-
                     context)))]
6            [valid-peers (peer-context-data-valid-peers peer-
             context)])
7        (set-subtract valid-peers current-connected-peers)))
```

4.2.1.5 Integrating Parts Together

The next procedure will ping all peers (that have connected to us or that we have connected to) in an attempt to sync blockchain data and update other stuff, such as the list of valid peers:

```
1    (define (peers/sync-data peer-context)
2      (define (loop)
```

```
3      (sleep 10)
4      (for [(p (peer-context-data-connected-peers peer-
       context))]
5        (let ([in (peer-info-io-input-port p)]
6              [out (peer-info-io-output-port p)])
7          (fprintf out "get-latest-blockchain\nget-valid-
           peers\n")
8          (flush-output out)))
9      (printf "Peer ~a reports ~a valid and ~a connected
       peers.\n"
10               (peer-context-data-name peer-context)
11               (set-count
12                 (peer-context-data-valid-peers peer-context))
13               (set-count
14                 (peer-context-data-connected-peers peer-
                   context)))
15     (loop))
16   (define t (thread loop))
17   (lambda ()
18     (kill-thread t)))
```

The following procedure is the entry point, where everything is launched together:

```
1    (define (run-peer peer-context)
2      (begin
3        (peers/serve peer-context)
4        (peers/connect peer-context)
5        (peers/sync-data peer-context)))
```

Finally, we export the necessary objects:

```
1   (provide (struct-out peer-context-data)
2             (struct-out peer-info)
3             run-peer)
```

4.2.2 Updating Existing Code

We need to modify main-helper.rkt to include the peer-to-peer
implementation:

```
1   ; ...
2   (require "peer-to-peer.rkt")
3   ; ...
4
5   (provide (all-from-out "blockchain.rkt")
6             (all-from-out "utils.rkt")
7             (all-from-out "peer-to-peer.rkt")
8             format-transaction print-block print-blockchain
                print-wallets)
```

4.2.3 The main-p2p.rkt File

This is where we will put all the components together and use them. We
want this implementation to accept some input arguments, such as the
blockchain database file and the IP and port addresses of each peer.

Once we create an executable, we have a way to pass input to it
by using the *command-line arguments*. For example, if our executable
is named blockchain, we can pass additional data to it by running
./blockchain <param1> <param2> <...>. Racket provides a built-in
procedure called current-command-line-arguments, which will read
these arguments into a vector (similar to a list), and we then use
vector->list to convert it to a list for further processing.

```
1   (require "main-helper.rkt")
2
3   (define args (vector->list  (current-command-line-
                                 arguments)))
4
5   (when (not (= 3 (length args)))
6     (begin
7       (printf "Usage: main-p2p.rkt db.data port
          ip1:port1,ip2:port2...")
8       (newline)
9       (exit)))
```

string-to-peer-info is a helper procedure that does additional parsing for the peers' information:

```
1   (define (string-to-peer-info s)
2     (let ([s (string-split s ":")])
3       (peer-info (car s) (string->number (cadr s)))))
```

We proceed by parsing the arguments:

```
1   (define db-filename (car args))
2   (define port (string->number (cadr args)))
3   (define valid-peers
4     (map string-to-peer-info (string-split (caddr args) ",")))
```

We then proceed with checking if the database file exists using file-exists?. This file will contain contents from a previous blockchain if it exists. If the file doesn't exist, we will proceed to create one.

```
1   (define db-blockchain
2     (if (file-exists? db-filename)
3         (file->struct db-filename)
4         (initialize-new-blockchain)))
```

We provide the functionality for creating a new blockchain:

```
1    (define wallet-a (make-wallet))
2
3    (define (initialize-new-blockchain)
4      (begin
5        (define coin-base (make-wallet))
6
7        (printf "Making genesis transaction...\n")
8        (define genesis-t (make-transaction coin-base wallet-a
         100 '()))
9
10       (define utxo (list
11                       (make-transaction-io 100 wallet-a)))
12
13       (printf "Mining genesis block...\n")
14       (define b (init-blockchain genesis-t "1337cafe" utxo))
15       b))
```

Next is the code for initialization of the current peer—it is named Test peer, and it contains data from the parsed command-line arguments (the port, valid peers, etc.).

```
1    (define peer-context
2      (peer-context-data "Test peer"
3                         port
4                         (list->set valid-peers)
5                         '()
6                         db-blockchain))
7    (define (get-blockchain) (peer-context-data-blockchain
     peer-context))
8
9    (run-peer peer-context)
```

We keep exporting the database to have up-to-date information whenever a user quits the app.

```
1   (define (export-loop)
2     (begin
3       (sleep 10)
4       (struct->file (get-blockchain) db-filename)
5       (printf "Exported blockchain to '~a'...\n" db-filename)
6       (export-loop)))
7
8   (thread export-loop)
```

Finally, we create a procedure to keep mining empty blocks. Note that the peer-to-peer implementation runs in threaded mode, so there will be no blocking if we keep running this procedure.

```
1    (define (mine-loop)
2      (let ([newer-blockchain
3             (send-money-blockchain (get-blockchain)
4                                    wallet-a
5                                    wallet-a
6                                    1
7                                    (file->contract "contract.
                                       script"))])
8        (set-peer-context-data-blockchain! peer-context newer-
           blockchain)
9        (printf "Mined a block!")
10       (sleep 5)
11       (mine-loop)))
12
13   (mine-loop)
```

We can proceed by creating an executable and share it with our friends. If we know their IP addresses (or they know ours), we can make a connection and thus form a system.

4.3 Summary

Congratulations! As part of this chapter, we added two new important features to the blockchain implementation: smart contracts and peer-to-peer support. This concludes the blockchain implementation of this book.

Conclusion

We've covered a bunch of stuff in this book. As a recap, we did the following:

- Section 1: We got a general high-level overview of the blockchain system.

- Section 2.3: We learned basic Lisp using the Racket (Scheme) dialect.

- Section 2.4: We created an executable with DrRacket.

- Section 3: We created a basic implementation of a blockchain that implements the structures and the operations for wallets, blocks, transactions, and digital signatures.

- Section 4.1: We implemented support for smart contracts.

- Section 4.2: We implemented support for peer-to-peer communication.

Here are some ideas for further development:

- Usually, a list of IP addresses and ports is contained in some public servers, but to keep things simple, we ignored that and implemented command-line parsing that accepts a list of IP addresses and ports. Ideally, we would create a simple server that maintains this list and shares it with peers that connect to the server, so that

© Boro Sitnikovski 2021
B. Sitnikovski, *Introducing Blockchain with Lisp*, https://doi.org/10.1007/978-1-4842-6969-5

the peers can get the list from a single place. Note that
the implementation is still decentralized; this public
server merely keeps a list of clients.

- Harden the security.

- Tweak the communication logic and the blockchain
  effort algorithms.

- Make the front-end more user-friendly.

In this book, we created a simple implementation of Bitcoin, but
the applications of blockchain are endless. There are many other ways
the technology can be leveraged, in general, using distributed data
management. More specifically, managing player's data in online
multiplayer games, or making an actual distributed database that uses a
subset of the blockchain's features.

We leave further extensions and implementations up to your
imagination.

Further Readings

Abelson, H., Sussman, J. G., *Structure and Interpretation of Computer Programs*, 2nd ed. 1996. The MIT Press. ISBN: 978-026-2510-875.

Friedman, P. D., Felleisen, M., Bibby, Duane. *The Little Schemer*, Fourth ed., 1995. The MIT Press. ISBN: 978-026-2560-993.

Nakamato, S., "Bitcoin: A Peer-to-Peer Electronic Cash System," 2008. `downloads.coindesk.com/research/whitepapers/bitcoin.pdf`.

The Racket Community, "The Racket Guide," 2014. `docs.racket-lang.org/guide/`.

APPENDIX A

Macros

So far we've been writing definitions for procedures and interacted with them, and we also interacted with some syntax, like quote, define, and so on. What if we had a way to write our own syntax? For example, could we write syntax that, when executed, would write code itself? Macros are a way to do exactly that.

---

❶ Definition A-1

A **macro** is a syntactic extension to a programming language. This means that we can write (or introduce our own) keywords into the programming language.

There is special syntax in Lisp, called define-macro, which allows us to create a macro. It accepts the name of a macro and its arguments (which are optional), and will return a quoted list of Lisp commands.

When we run our definitions (or compile them), Racket will replace all occurrences of the macro call with the actual output that it produces.

As an example, if we have the following macro (define-macro (add-one x) (list '+ x 1)), wherever we write (add-one x), it will be replaced with the expression (+ x 1).

Macros are all about affecting how the evaluation model works. Racket has an eager evaluation model, which means that all expressions will be evaluated at a given time on a procedure call. For macros, on the other hand, since Racket will replace the code before evaluating it, expressions will be evaluated only when needed.

The following example illustrates the difference between a macro and a procedure. Consider the following definitions:

```
1   (require compatibility/defmacro)
2
3   (define-macro (our-if-macro a b c)
4     (list 'cond (list a b) (list 'else c)))
5
6   (define (our-if-procedure a b c)
7     (cond (a b) (else c)))
```

With a few evaluations:

```
1   > (our-if-macro (eq? '() '()) #t #f)
2   #t
3   > (our-if-procedure (eq? '() '()) #t #f)
4   #t
5   > (our-if-macro  (eq? '() '()) (display "True")
    (display "False"))
6   True
7   > (our-if-procedure (eq? '() '()) (display "True")
    (display "False"))
8   TrueFalse
```

We can notice a couple of things from this code:

- We required a library that contains the define-macro syntax.

- We implemented our own if both as a macro and as a procedure.

- In the interactions area, we used a procedure called display, which prints stuff to the output.

- We see that the macro and the procedure produce two different outputs.

The macro and the procedure behave differently, as expected. However, in the case of if, it makes sense to implement it as a macro rather than as a procedure. Since Racket has an eager evaluation model, it will evaluate all arguments, but it does not make sense to evaluate the else case if we are sure that the first case will match.

Let's manually expand the macro to get a feel for how it really works.

```
1   (our-if-macro (eq? '() '()) #t #f)
2   = (list 'cond (list (eq? '() '()) #t) (list 'else #f))
3   = (list 'cond (list #t #t) (list 'else #f))
4   = '(cond (#t #t) (else #f))
```

That is, the macro returns a quoted expression that's supposed to be evaluated once the macro has been used.

The way we've written our macro makes things much more explicit in terms of execution and substitution. We can also write it as follows, which is a bit more implicit, where the backtick is like a quote mark (quasiquote) and the comma is like an unquote mark (the opposite of quote):

```
1   (define-macro (our-if-macro a b c)
2     `(cond (,a ,b) (else ,c)))
```

Hygienic Macros

The way we wrote the macros earlier is not good practice in Racket. Consider the following example:

```
1   (define-macro (swap a b)
2     `(let ((tmp ,a))
```

```
3           (set! ,a ,b)
4           (set! ,b tmp)))
```

This looks like a perfectly safe macro. Indeed:

```
1   > (define x 1)
2   > (define y 2)
3   > (displayln  (list x y))
4   (1 2)
5   > (swap x y)
6   > (displayln (list x y))
7   (2 1)
```

However, we can break it with the following code:

```
1   > (define x 1)
2   > (define tmp 2)
3   > (displayln (list x tmp))
4   (1 2)
5   > (swap x tmp)
6   > (displayln (list x tmp))
7   (1 2)
```

To see what happened, we can expand the macro by hand. The macro translates to:

```
1   > `(let ((tmp ,x))
2        (set! ,x ,tmp)
3        (set! ,tmp tmp))
4   '(let ((tmp 2)) (set! 2 2) (set! 2 tmp))
```

In this case, tmp was already defined (using define) and was reused in the body of the let. As we can see, it is hard to control the accidental capture of local identifiers. We can get around the problem by using gensym, which returns a unique symbol every time it's called:

```
1    (define-macro (swap a b)
2      (let ((tmp (gensym)))
3        `(let ((,tmp ,a))
4           (set! ,a ,b)
5           (set! ,b ,tmp))))
```

Now our macro works as intended:

```
1    > (define x 1)
2    > (define tmp 2)
3    > (displayln (list x tmp))
4    (1 2)
5    > (swap x tmp)
6    > (displayln (list x tmp))
7    (1 2)
```

However, instead of gensym, we can use define-syntax-rules, which is the preferred way in Racket.

```
1    (define-syntax-rule (swap a b)
2      (let ((tmp a))
3        (set! a b)
4        (set! b tmp)))
```

This syntax will create a hygienic macro that does not have the issues that define-macro has.

For another example, let's create a macro that will allow us to run some command infinitely:

```
1    (define-syntax-rule (loop f)
2      (letrec ([fix (lambda (k) (k) (fix k))])
3        (fix (lambda () f))))
```

Note that, if loop was a procedure instead, then (loop (displayln "test")) would not have worked since it would have evaluated the call to displayln right away. We had to pass (lambda () (displayln "test")) as a trick to defer evaluation, and then use fix to keep evaluating this lambda over and over.

The loop macro allows us to do (loop (print (eval (read) ns)))— note the REPL acronym. The expression eval <...> ns will try to evaluate the expression <...> in the ns namespace/context. To get the base (initial) namespace, we can use the make-base-namespace procedure. In this case, the namespace will be initially empty, but it may be extended with variables or procedures, depending on which commands are executed.

```
1   > (define ns (make-base-namespace))
2   > (loop (print (eval (read) ns)))
3   (+ 1 1)
4   2(define x 5)
5   #<void>(+ 2 x)
6   7
```

The printing is a bit off because it is missing newlines. If we use displayln in place of print, it will produce much more readable output:

```
1   > (define ns (make-base-namespace))
2   > (loop (displayln (eval (read) ns)))
3   (+ 1 1)
4   2
5   (define x 5)
6   #<void>
7   (+ 2 x)
8   7
```

Index

A

Abstraction, 22
Abstract syntax tree, 24–26
Asymmetric algorithm, 11
Asymmetric-key algorithm, 12

B

Bitcoin, 16, 17
Blockchain
    definitions, 2
    encryption and
        decryption, 8–14
blockchain.data file, 99
blockchain.rkt file
    construction, 74
    Hashcash algorithm, 77–79
    hashing and verification, 75, 76
    initialization, 91
    rewards, 92
    transaction adding, 92–94
    verification, 95

C

Centralized place, 4
Command-line arguments, 128
Composition, 22

Conditional procedures, 42–45
Construct, 36
Crypto factory, 85
Current-command-line-
        arguments, 128

D

Data structure, 21
Decentralized ledger, 6
Decryption, 8
define-macro syntax, 138
define-syntax-rules, 141
Deserialization, 70
Digital signatures, 4, 13, 86
Double-spending problem, 3
DrRacket, 29

E

Encryption and decryption
        asymmetric-key algorithm, 11, 12
        function, 9
        symmetric-key algorithm, 10, 11
Executable, 66

F

Functions, 9

© Boro Sitnikovski 2021
B. Sitnikovski, *Introducing Blockchain with Lisp*, https://doi.org/10.1007/978-1-4842-6969-5

Printed in the United States
by Baker & Taylor Publisher Services